10699492

The Trapnall Legacy

The Trapnall Legacy

Jan Calloway

This book is made possible by the Arkansas Commemorative Commission, Trapnall Hall, and funded by receipts of the rental program at Trapnall Hall.

ACKNOWLEDGMENTS

Without the help, encouragement and criticism of many people, this work would never have made it to final form. I owe many thanks to:

Barbara Brigance, the best boss around, and Facility Manager of Trapnall Hall

Margaret Ross, Arkansas Gazette Historian

Carolyn Grimes, Harrodsburg Historical Society

Dr. John L. Ferguson, State Historian

Lucy Robinson, Director, Arkansas Commemorative Commission

Russell Baker, Archivist, and the patient staff of the Arkansas History Commission

Tom Dillard, Historical Parks Planner, Department of Parks and Tourism

Brian Austin, Trapnel Family Historian, Staffordshire, England

The many court clerks who took time to correspond, especially *Gladys Hicks,* Chicot County Clerk

Reverend Chester King, Harrodsburg, Kentucky, St. Phillips Episcopal Church

Wilson Stiles, Architectural Historian

Garnett Mullis, Development Director, Old State House.

Sandra Taylor Smith

Mrs. George Rose (Peg) Smith

Rita Pascall Wooley

Rita Anderson, Archival Assistant, University of Arkansas for Medical Sciences

Butch Miller, photographer

Holly Gilliland, loyal friend

Jim Watkins, Exhibit Specialist, Old State House

My picky friend . . .

Trapnall Hall   circa 1915

TABLE OF CONTENTS

Trapnall Hall   circa 1920

PROLOGUE

The story reaches almost the height of a classical tragedy; a handsome well-educated young man of a distinguished family background marries his love and moves to the new territories to seek fame and fortune. He finds both, but dies suddenly at the apex of his career. His legacy to us is a fine home, several mysteries and a new state's deep appreciation for the talents he shared to help form her and mold her into what she is today.

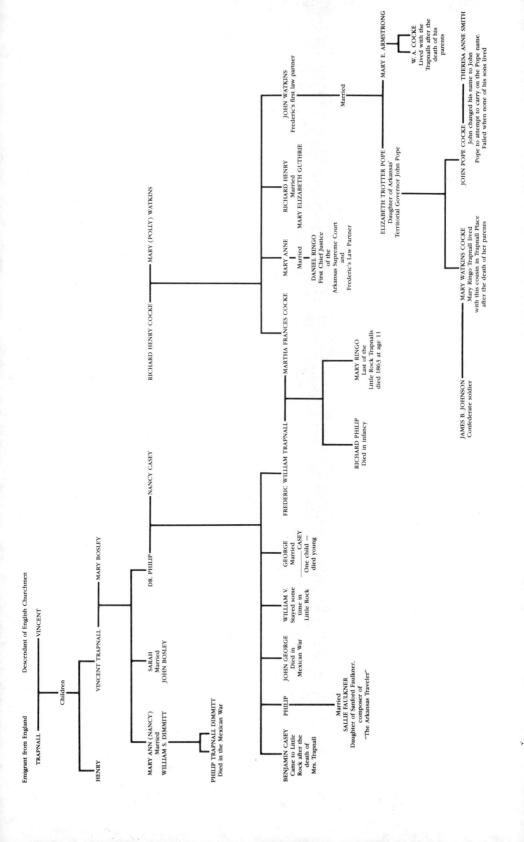

Chapter I

ANCESTRY

On May 23, 1807, in Harrodsburg, Kentucky, Frederic W. Trapnall was born to Dr. Philip and Nancy Casey Trapnall.[1] He was the first child of the couple.

Throughout his life, Frederic had a strong tie to his ancestry. The earliest reference to the name Trapnall is from 1187 near the village of Pilton, which is near Glastonbury, England, the Avalon of Arthurian legend. When the French-speaking secretaries taking census wrote the name they spelled it "Tropinel". When an Englishman wrote it circa 1220, the name was "Troppenhule", meaning "of the village on the hill."

The first use of the simplified Trapnel, the spelling which has lasted in England, was circa 1470. The American branch of the family changed the spelling to Trapnall in the 18th century. The earliest known American reference concerns John Trapnall of Exeter who was trading to Newfoundland in 1684.[2]

Frederic's great-grandfather was an emigrant from Staffordshire, England, where the Trapnell family still is today. He came to the Colonies in a very early period of their development[3].

Frederic's grandfather, Vincent Trapnall (the spelling was altered from Trapnel to Trapnall in the 18th century by the family) was a farmer in Baltimore County, Maryland. On November 20, 1768, he married Mary Bosley.[4] Their son, born on January 4, 1773, was Philip Trapnall. They also had two daughters, Sarah and Mary Ann, sometimes called Nancy. The daughters both married: Mary Ann in 1796 to William S. Dimmitt and Sarah, after the move to Harrodsburg, to Dr. John Bosley, a distant cousin from Harrodsburg. Mary Ann and her husband died early in life after having two sons and a daughter.[5]

Frederic's father was a lineal descendant through his grandmother of the Vincent family. They included ministers of the established Church of England. William Vincent was Bishop of London; Philip Vincent was Bishop of Durham; Admiral Vincent was a distinguished officer of the Navy.[6] These names, William, Philip, Vincent, were passed down to many male members of the family.

Map of Kentucky

Chapter II

FAMILY

At the age of fourteen, Frederic's father Philip was sent to Annapolis to complete his preliminary education. His medical training was completed in the spring of 1796, when he graduated from the University of Pennsylvania. He associated himself in Hagerstown, Maryland with Dr. Frederick Dorsey and established a successful practice.[1] He remained in practice at Hagerstown for two years where he was "one of the Incorporators of the Medical and Chirugical Society of Maryland which was passed at the State Assembly January 20, 1799."[2]

In the fall of 1800, he moved to Harrodsburg, Kentucky, the fulfillment of a wish that Dr. Philip had long indulged.

Harrodsburg, the "birthplace of Kentucky," is located in central Kentucky on the fringes of bluegrass country.

Here, Dr. Philip met and on July 24, 1806, married Nancy Casey, daughter of Peter Casey of Fountain Blue, Mercer County, Kentucky.[3] Caseyville, a prosperous town on the Ohio River in Union County, was named for this family. Dr. Philip's wife was described as "a lady of high cultivation and intellect and of great prudence, who was truly a help-meet to him and with whom he lived forty-five years, raising a large and respectable family."[4]

Vincent Trapnall, Philip's father, apparently followed his son to Harrodsburg. The 1810 census lists Vincent as head of the household composed of himself, his wife Mary, Dr. Philip and his wife of four years, Nancy, and their three-year-old son Frederic, eight slaves and one "free person," perhaps a field worker or a visiting cousin.

Dr. Philip had been in Harrodsburg for five years when the people of Mercer County elected him to a seat in the Legislature of the Commonwealth. He served two terms, 1805-6 and 1806-7, with such distinguished colleagues as Henry Clay and John Pope, future Governor of Arkansas Territory.[5] In these sessions of the legislature, Dr. Philip served on several committees concerning inspections of beef and pork and repeal of an act incorporating the Kentucky Insurance Company.[6]

Other concerns of his included consideration of public claims, examination of the treasurer's office and collection of monies due the commonwealth from counties. During both terms he served on a standing committee concerning elections and privileges. He presented a bill to improve the navigation of the Kentucky River. He was an uncompromising Whig whose political opinions would be reflected later by his son Frederic in the Arkansas General Assembly. In 1812, he ran for Congress but was defeated by Samuiel McKee of Lancaster.[7]

Dr. Philip's medical practice was as successful in Harrodsburg as it had been in Hagerstown. It was said "by those intimately acquainted with his practice that he possessed remarkable insight into the nature and character of diseases, was remarkably accurate in his diagnosis, and rarely ever mistaken in the judgment he formed."[8] His "masculine vigor of intellect and superior literary and professional attainments"[9] placed him in the front ranks of his profession.

Philip was described by friends as "a handsome man with an intelligent face, but a countenance and expression that was forbidding to those who did not know how to read it."[10] He was devoted to his friends to the point of idolatry, and would make almost any sacrifice for their accommodation; but he was as implacable toward his enemies as he was ardent toward his friends.[11] He was so overwhelming a personality that some went to the extent of calling him eccentric. A close associate says he was "... not fully prepared to acquit him of that charge. There was something remarkably striking in his person and manners."[12] One of his ancestors, Admiral Vincent, was so tall and commanding in his person and possessed such an air of majesty that his very appearance excited a feeling of awe in friends, and struck terror into his enemies.[13] A large physical stature and majestic air seem to have been a characteristic of the Vincent family which Dr. Philip and his son inherited. Dr. Philip was a full and very straight 6'2". He was a muscular man with a large and very long nose. This prominent feature was also handed down to his sons. The doctor wore a green silk patch over one eye. He lost his eye in a duel with Dr. Bybee, a cousin. Although we cannot be sure of the cause of the fight, one source states the trouble was over some Negroes.[14] After this loss, Dr. Philip never allowed his portrait painted or picture taken, which explains why we have no portrait of this man. Perhaps he passed this reluctance down to his son, as well, for we have no likeness of Frederic, only rumors of a long lost portrait.

Philip Trapnall served in his chosen profession for twenty-two brilliant years. In 1818, he retired, divided his awesome and well selected library among his young friends and established himself upon a farm.[15]

He had always been an active member of the Episcopal Church and after his retirement the thoughts of Dr. Philip's active mind turned even more to religious matters. In 1818-19, he wrote articles in defense of the doctrines of his church which were published and replied to by Dr. C. Calland.[16]

After retirement the doctor also entertained frequently, for which "his

4

fine conversational power and open hospitality eminently fitted him."[17]

By 1820, there were twenty-five people in Dr. Philip's household. Ten were slaves; ten were men from below ten to over forty-five; five were women.[18] The doctor's attitude toward one of his slaves is expressed in a reference in his will to "my faithful servant Dick, or rather humble Friend." This will gave Dick his freedom, and the Doctor's clothes and ax. He was asked to stay with the boys until the estate was wound up, as any good friend would do.[19]

Doctor Philip and his wife Nancy reared a family of six sons: Frederick William, John George, William Vincent, Benjamin Casey, George and Philip.[20] There is a rich oral tradition in Harrodsburg concerning the Trapnalls who are remembered as devoted churchmen and as important citizens in the early days of Kentucky's first town.

Nancy Casey Trapnall is described as a woman of uncommon good sense, business efficiency and unparalleled popularity of manner.[21] In Daviess' *History of Mercer and Boyle Counties*, a sketch of John B. Thompson states:

> John had his study and play under several teachers in the Academy on old Ford Hill, and then some rollicking times with the Daviess and Marshall and Trapnel boys, where Dr. Trapnel [sic] always kept a first rate teacher, who in John's time, was Dr. Daly, an educated Irishman, whose speciality was mathematics. To that place he always looked back as an oasis, never forgetting the motherly spirit with which that princess of good women bore with the mischief of a score of boys, of which he and his brother, Henry, were two. These brothers took their finishing course with Dr. Polin, a graduate of Dublin University.[22]

With his numerous sons and several slaves, Dr. Philip raised hay, corn, Irish potatoes, wheat, rye and flax. His livestock included sheep, pigs, bulls and cows, as well as horses.[23] Some of these horses were of very fine stock. A large bay horse was listed on the inventory of the estate worth $150, a goodly amount in those times.

John George Trapnall, the second son of Philip and Nancy was an early adventurer to Texas in the 1840s - before the Mexican War.[24] He was captured by the Mexicans and imprisoned in the Castle of Perote. In the January 16, 1844, edition of the *Arkansas Banner* is an article which reprints a letter from Judge Edward Cross and reply from Secretary of State A. P. Upshur. Judge Cross had written the president asking for information and for his interference on behalf of "a young gentleman, related to a highly respectable citizen of our State who is one of the Texan prisoners in Mexico."[25] The paper reports that "Many other citizens of the State have relatives and friends in the same unfortunate condition, and will rejoice to learn that there is prospect of their release at an early date."[26] Mr. Upshur's reply "upon the subject of Mr. Trapnall, one of the Texan prisoners in Mexico," states, "A recent dispatch from General Thompson, the Minister of the U.S. in that country represents that it was expected all those prisoners would soon be released."[27] In spite of these assurances, John died in the Castle of Perote.[28] A nephew of Dr. Philip, named for him,

St. Philip's Church window dedications

Philip Trapnall Dimmitt, (son of Dr. Philip's sister Mary Ann and her husband William S. Dimmitt) had apparently died there earlier in 1841.[29]

There is early mention in the *Arkansas Gazette* of another of Frederic's brothers, William Vincent Trapnall, born in 1817. On the Fourth of July, 1839, a holiday widely celebrated with speeches, parades, dinners, songs, music and gun salutes, a volunteer toast at a dinner at City Hotel in Little Rock was given by W. P. Trapnall (probably a misprint for W. V.). The toast was "Liberty and union, now and forever, one and inseparable."[30] Albert Pike read a poem on this occasion; Major Robert W. Johnson read the Declaration of Independence; the orator of the Day was John W. Cocke, Frederic's brother-in-law and law partner.[31] No doubt Frederic also attended although he is not mentioned in any of the reports. William was perhaps visiting Frederic and his wife. In 1850 when W. V. Trapnal was thirty-three, he is listed in the Kentucky Census for Union County, where he was working as a lawyer.[32] He died in Mercer County about 1867, unmarried and intestate.[33]

One of the most notable of Frederic's brothers was Benjamin Casey Trapnall who was born in 1819, one year after his father retired to his farm in Mercer. Benjamin stayed in Harrodsburg for most of his life, although he did spend a few years in Little Rock after the Civil War.

Benjamin is described as an "accomplished gentlemen" who resembled Frederic "in person and in manner."[34] Davies describes him as "a lawyer of fine personal appearance and pleasing address."[35] Ben began his law practice in 1840, in Mercer County.[36] In 1857, he was elected to represent Mercer County as his father had, in the Kentucky House of Representatives. He served for two terms.[37]

In 1857-59, Ben took a major part in the only military event of the period. The Governor was empowered by the Kentucky legislature on February 15, 1857, to raise volunteer troops to go to Utah.[38] Captain Benjamin Trapnall raised a company of volunteers to help "suppress the rebellion" in Utah.[39]

Brigham Young had been appointed Territorial Governor of Utah by President Fillmore in 1850, and then had driven out Federal Judges when they refused to agree with him. In 1857-58, President Buchanan sent a new governor in with an army troop to support him. The Governor of Kentucky accepted Benjamin Trapnall's troop, but they were never called out. Perhaps they could have been used though, since Brigham Young's scorched-earth strategy was finally successful against the Federal troops, and they obtained nominal submission at best.[40]

Like other members of his family, Benjamin was actively involved in the Episcopal church. He was one of the incorporators of St. Philip's Church in Harrodsburg in 1861. The church, one of the best exterior and interior examples of Gothic architecture in the central part of the United States, was listed on the National Register of Historic Places in 1978.[41]

Two of the five beautiful stained-glass lancet windows from England that are in the church are dedicated to Nancy Trapnall and Dr. Philip Trapnall. The type of glass used for these windows is no longer produced in such quality anywhere.[42]

The church came into serious financial difficulties before its building's completion during the Civil War. G. D. Runyan, a close friend of the Trapnall family, bought the church building at Ben's suggestion, to pay off creditors.[43]

Another brother who has an interesting history, closely tied to Frederic's, is his youngest brother Philip, born in 1827. He will be discussed in more detail in Chapter XIV.

Frederic was the eldest child of Philip and Nancy, born May 23, 1807,[44] an exact ten months after the marriage of his parents during Dr. Philip's service in the Kentucky House of Representatives.

When Frederic was eleven, Dr. Philip retired to his farm in Harrodsburg. We have pictured already Frederic's childhood among a score of brothers, a successful father and genteel mother.

The home which, legend has it, was the old Trapnall home in Harrodsburg still stands, although it has been extensively changed. The house rests on a large tree-shaded plot south of Harrodsburg. The Greek Revival style of architecture was at its peak in Kentucky the first half of the nineteenth century. It is likely that at the time of its construction, the house was Greek Revival in design.

Sheathed in aluminum siding now the house retains some degree of its original design. Distant parallels to Frederick's future home in Little Rock are found in the entrance door trim, the classic columns supporting the portico and the basic plan of the structure itself.

There is no record of Frederic's early education except for the general references already mentioned. Daviess' *History of Mercer and Boyle Counties* says of the education of those men raised in the young Commonwealth of Kentucky:

> But I know the first generation of Kentucky
> men, at least professional men, has as good a
> classical education as their college bred sons,
> i.e. has Mathematics, Greek, and Latin for
> their courses. Natural science was ignored, and
> the general intelligence of each individual
> depended a good deal on observation and
> contact with other men and precarious access
> to books.[45]

Although Frederic was not exactly of the first generation of Kentuckians, it appears that he was not educated at a college as was his youngest brother Philip. Philip graduated from Bacon College.[46]

For his primary education Frederic probably went to Fry's Academy in Mercer "in whose halls," Maria Daviess says, "the prominent lawyers of Kentucky took their finishing courses, though probably some of the wealthier students went back to the old states for a diploma."[47] Fry's Academy was one of the best primary schools and one of the closest to Frederic's home.

Dr. Trapnall was very active in the importation of educators for the centers of learning, possibly because of the sons he had to educate. It was in their interests that he imported Mr. Daley, a prominent educator. Later there was Dr. Polin, an Irish graduate of Dublin University who taught in Harrodsburg and was most successful.[48] But again to quote Ms. Daviess, "good as schools may be, one fact is patent to all generations, that men and women can only educate themselves."[49]

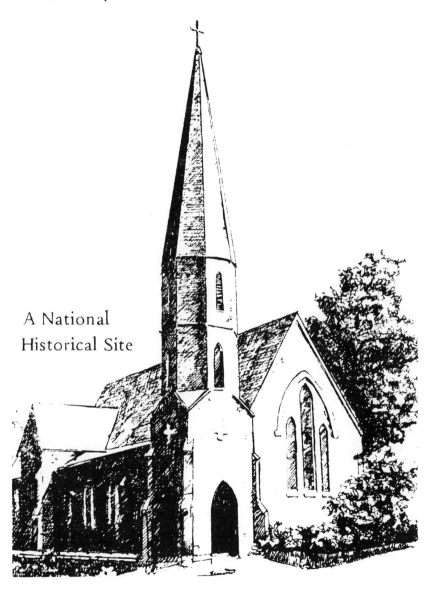

A National Historical Site

St. Philip's Church in Harrodsburg, Kentucky

9

Nazareth Academy in Nazareth, Kentucky

Chapter III

SPRINGFIELD

Frederic moved to nearby Springfield in 1829, possibly to apprentice himself to another lawyer.[1] He had friends in Springfield already, and he had stood as bondsman for James N. Cocke and Lucy G. Fry at their marriage on September 10, 1828,[2] in Springfield.

In 1835, Mr. Trapnall presented a case in the Kentucky Supreme Court which had first been tried in the Marion County Court. He won the case, but this may not have been a significant accomplishment, since he appeared for the plaintiff and the defendant had no lawyer.[3]

In 1834, the voters of Washington County, Kentucky, elected Frederic to a seat in the Commonwealth's House of Representatives. The session began on December 31, 1834. William Conway who would also later come to Arkansas served in this same legislature from Hardin County.

Frederic had many concerns in this session of the legislature. Several of the bills he presented and committees on which he served concerned the courts and the method of summoning jurors and providing for their compensation. Others concerned internal improvements, such as the petition of Marion County citizens asking for a ferry, incorporation of the Lebanon Male and Female Academy and creation of the Springfield and Bardstown Turnpike Road Company.

One of the most interesting bills he presented was to "remove the disabilities of *infant femes covert.*"[4] We do not know the source of Frederic's interest in the legal rights of minor married women, but more than a year later, he married a sixteen-year-old.

Frederic met his future wife, Martha Francis Cocke, in Springfield. Miss Cocke had attended Nazareth Academy in Nazareth, Kentucky.[5] Her parents were the late Richard Henry Cocke and Polly Watkins Cocke, who had died within three days of each other in 1823.[6]

Frederic and Martha married on the first of November in 1836. It was the bride's sixteenth birthday as well as her wedding day.

Steamboat receipt: Trapnall probate file

Chapter IV

ARRIVAL IN EARLY LITTLE ROCK

Almost immediately after their marriage, the couple made the journey to Little Rock. Arkansas was still sparsely settled and had left behind its territorial status in that year. However, life in Arkansas did have much to recommend it.

The new Mrs. Trapnall had many connections in the frontier town of Little Rock, some of them very close ties in the upper political, business and social strata of the city.

Martha's brother, John Watkins Cocke, had been married in 1829 to Elizabeth Trotter Pope, the daughter of Arkansas' Territorial Governor John Pope and his second wife Eliza J. D. Johnson. John and Elizabeth Cocke had two children: John Pope Cocke and Mary Watkins Cocke. Their son changed his name in the latter years of his life to John Pope at the request of Governor Pope, his grandfather, who wanted the name Pope to continue. This proved to be a futile gesture. John Pope (Cocke) and his wife had nine children, only two of whom were sons. The first, named John Pope, died in infancy in 1860. The second, also named John Pope, was born October 19, 1863, and died in 1875.[1]

Mrs. Trapnall's sister-in-law, Mrs. Elizabeth Pope Cocke, died near Springfield, Kentucky on May 1, 1835. Eight years later John W. Cocke married Mary E. Armstrong. They had one son, W. A. Cocke, in 1843. The young boy's parents died soon after his birth - Mrs. Cocke in February 1847, and John W. in October 1849. (John W. was buried in Little Rock, but later his body was taken back to his boyhood state of Kentucky and reburied in St. Rose Churchyard, Springfield.[2]) W. A. Cocke lived with the Trapnalls for the rest of his brief life.[3] Perhaps he helped to fill the place of the Trapnalls' son Richard Phillip who had died in infancy on June 9, 1841.[4] W. A. Cocke died on September 10, 1853, at the age of ten, and is buried in the Trapnall family plot at Mount Holly Cemetery in Little Rock.[5]

Her brother was not Mrs. Trapnall's only connection with Little Rock. Her eldest sister, Mary Ann Cocke, who had also attended Nazareth Academy[6], was married to a Little Rock lawyer, Daniel Ringo. Daniel Ringo had been appointed the first Chief Justice of the Arkansas Supreme

Court in September 1836. No doubt these relations helped to ease the shock of moving to a new state. A community of former Kentuckians were already in Little Rock. Among them were Robert Crittenden, John Pope, William Conway and James B. Johnson.

As the Trapnalls arrived in Little Rock, they found a thriving, growing frontier town. Arkansas was considered a frontier state because its western border was on unorganized territory.[7] In 1836, "on the eve of statehood," the *Arkansas Advocate* published the official census of 726 in the city.[8] Little Rock had grown rapidly from 1830 when it had a population of only 430.[9] Albert Pike in his "Letters from Arkansas" in *American Monthly Magazine* described Little Rock in 1830.

> Little Rock ... is laid off with tolerable regularity by streets running at right angles ... The houses are a motley mixture; consisting of every variety, from brick blocks of two stories to log cabins.[10]

By 1835 Pike's opinion and his description of Little Rock had both greatly changed.

> There is not a more agreeable town anywhere than Little Rock. Its citizens are men from all parts of the Union, and there is no more intelligent, shrewd, and sensible, and at the same time generous and hospitable community in the world.[11]

The steamboat was very influential, in the growth of Little Rock. The *Eagle* was the first steamer to make it to Little Rock in 1822.[12] For the next ten years, only a few captains would brave the rough Arkansas River; one boat per week was average during the months that the river could be traversed. But around 1830, traffic began to increase. The *Gazette* was filled with merchants' advertisements after the arrival of a steamboat which would restock their supplies of coffee, brandy, almonds, candy, tobacco, flour, crackers, apples, ale, seafood, wine, etc.

Little Rock was in touch with the news in this early period through its two newspapers, William Woodruff's *Arkansas Gazette* and Charles Bertrand's *Advocate*. The *Advocate* was printed from 1830 through 1844. The *Arkansas Gazette* has been in continuous publication since 1819, except during the last twenty months of the Civil War.

A Little Rock Debating Society sponsored public debates,[13] and a racetrack with a spectator grandstand provided entertainment. Races were held during the first week in November with schedules and descriptions of races in the paper. The racetrack and jockey club was located on the spot now occupied by the Little Rock Arsenal. An amateur Thalian Society presented plays and donated its surplus funds to charity.[14] In 1838, a professional theatre troupe came to the city. Its first season was considered a success by the *Arkansas Gazette*.[15]

Little Rock's mail was delivered and received from Memphis three times a week in 1835. It usually took two weeks to receive the Washington and Baltimore papers.[16] Occasionally local citizens brought other papers, especially Kentucky ones, to local newspaper offices, which reprinted interesting items. One example of this occurs in the March 3, 1835, *Arkansas Gazette.* An article is reprinted from a Lexington paper describing a fatal accident in the trial run of a new locomotive. Lewis Lonkard, of Lexington, had been instantly killed; Leonard Taylor, of Lexington, and Daniel Green, of Fayette had each a leg broken; W. A. Cocke and Joseph Holt of Louisville and F. W. Trapnall, of Springfield, had been severely bruised.[17]

Little Rock had educational facilities for members of both sexes by 1830. A school for young ladies was run by Mrs. Lucy E. West. She promised "a good English education and plain and ornamental needlework." Her terms - spelling, reading, writing, arithmetic, per quarter $4.00; grammar, geography, history, rhetoric, and needlework $5.00. Parents of prospective students were assured that "the strictest attention will be paid to their morals,"[18] (a condition not mentioned in advertisements for the education of the young men.)

Trapnall later supported many different educational facilities in Little Rock, although he had no children old enough to go to school. He donated money to St. John's College, the first institution of higher learning in Arkansas when it first began. He was on the board of visitors of Little Rock High School, a Boarding and Day School for Young Ladies which proposed to make French the language always spoken at the school since it was considered indispensible to a polite education. At this school the young ladies could study, along with more usual subjects, harp, oriental painting, Japan work, inlaying of ebony and ivory, Hamburg work, wax flowers, singing and a choice of four languages.[19]

Christ Episcopal Church, where Trapnall was a Vestryman, also began a school in 1852, under the direction of the Rector Rev. A. F. Freeman and the Wardens of the church.

The Trapnalls arrived only a few months after the first session of the legislature met in September of 1836, in the almost completed capitol building.

James S. Conway had been elected Governor for a four-year term at the same time Daniel Ringo was elected Chief Justice. The legislature elected all state officers except the governor and the judges of the Supreme and Circuit Courts.

The Trapnalls may have lived with the Ringos for some time after their arrival in Arkansas. There is no record of their place of residence prior to 1843.

By the 1840 census they were listed in their own home, the location of which is not known. They had a total of seven slaves, three men and four women, to support the household. The household also had two men between the ages of twenty and thirty engaged in the "learned professions."[20] Possibly the second man was Frederic's brother William Vincent, still visiting as he had been on the Fourth of July in 1839.

On June 9, 1841, the first child of Frederic and Martha died in infancy. No birthdate is given for this son, who was named Richard Philip Trapnall after his two grandfathers.[21]

Chapter V

BEGINNING OF LEGAL PRACTICE

Frederic Trapnall quickly became a successful lawyer and politician in the new state. The following newspaper story shows how he was seen by his contemporaries.

> The attention of the House is arrested by a soft, fluent voice, falling in clear accents, and well turned periods, from the lips of the speaker. A tall handsome proportioned son of Kentucky is upon the floor. The size and shape of the head, the well developed and strongly marked features, afforded the strongest indications of more than ordinary intellect. The attitude and gesticulation are graceful, and a good natured smile plays upon the large and well-formed mouth. The appearance, manner and peculiarly happy exordium of the speaker are well calculated to attract attention. The comprehension is strong, perception clear, and mode of argument exceeding plausible. Mr. Trapnall of Pulaski wields a polished blade. As an orator he has but few equals in the state. He is distinguished as a lawyer and a gentleman of intelligence. As a politician he is a Whig of the deepest dye, and the most active leader of his party in Arkansas.[1]

One of the first recorded actions of Frederic Trapnall in Arkansas is his participation in the founding of the first Bar Association of the State. The constitution of the Bar Association was "Adopted at an aggregate meeting of the Profession, held in the city of Little Rock, on the 24th day of November, 1837."[2] At a meeting of the Association held January 15, 1838, the nineteen members passed and signed a set of resolutions. The roster of members includes Chester Ashley, John H. Clendenin, J. W. Cocke, William Conway, Edward Cross, Absalom Fowler, S. H. Hempstead, Albert Pike, William C. Scott, George Watkins and F. W. Trapnall.[3] Only three were not from Little Rock: William McK. Ball from Fayetteville, Nathan Haggard from Batesville and William B. R. Horner from Helena. Hallum refers to many of these lawyers as "men who would have done honor to the profession in any state, and who have never been excelled in the history of the Arkansas Bar."[4] Pope says, "Few, if any of the new states could boast such an array of legal and oratorical talent and ability."[5]

The objectives of the Association are stated in the Second Section of Article I. They are threefold: "to promote courtesy and kindness in the intercourse of its members, to establish uniformity in certain points of professional conduct, and to protect generally the interests and dignity of the bar."[6]

The members were selective about who could join the Association. Counsellors and attorneys-at-law who wished to join the Bar applied to one of the regular members, who referred the application to the Committee on Membership, which reported to the Association. The vote was *viva voce* and had to be unanimous. Meetings were held semi-annually; members dined and heard guest speakers at the meetings. Judges or visiting accredited members of the profession were invited to attend.

Article IV of the Constitution concerned the conduct of the members. There were admonitions against lending money or property to any suitor or client, or acting in any "of the relations of life in a manner unbecoming a gentleman."[7] The consequences of such action were severe. For a first transgression, the offender suffered a reprimand by the president in the presence of the Association; for the second he was expelled from the Bar. Once expelled a member could "in no instance be recognized as the professional peer or social companion of any member of this Association."[8]

Article VI contained rates of compensation and fees for a number of services.

For verbal advice	$5.00
For written advice	$10.00
For Wills	$20.00
For filing brief or arguing each case in the Supreme Court	$25.00 [9]

In keeping with the gentlemanly spirit of the court, members were warned not to "indulge in any remark, or course of conduct, calculated to affect the reputation or wound the feelings of his competitor in the cause; but on all occasions members shall scrupulously observe towards each other at the bar, the most marked courtesy and cordiality of bearing."[10]

The resolutions passed at what was probably the second meeting of the Association, included arrangements for collecting the membership fee of $10 annually, and the association's intention to use any money left after expenses to begin a library of books of law reports or works on jurisprudence. They also record the organization's resolve to petition the legislature for an appropriation for procuring a law library.

Pope, in his history of early Arkansas, paints for us a vivid picture of what a young lawyer in the new state of Arkansas had to face.

The early days of the State were especially prolific in men of eminent legal ability. It is to be very much doubted if the present day can show so large an array of first class forensic talent, to say nothing of the question of profound thought, deep research and acquaintance with authorities, and almost unerring judgment in arriving at just and wise conclusions.

To be sure, the field was not so wide, nor the concerns so varied as now, still the multitudinous questions which were constantly being brought before the courts were such as would naturally grow out of the unsettled state of affairs of a new country, and the transition from the Territorial period to Statehood. These questions, which were often of a very complex nature, taxed the ability of counsel to unravel and courts to settle. There was but little mediocre talent on the bench or at the bar in those early days, nor was there any easy and quickly trodden path to preferment in the profession. It was not sufficient that the would-be lawyer have a copy of the statutes under one arm and the code under the other, and but very little of either in his head, to enable him to pass the required ordeal for license to practice. It was also a very difficult matter for a young and untried lawyer to rise in his profession. He had an apprenticeship to serve and had to be content, at first, with what was tendered him from his master's table, so to speak. But his reward came in time, when, after much study and preparation, and the practice of great patience, which was about all the practice the most of them had for several years, they were invited to come up higher and enjoy their reward, which was usually ample when once a footing was obtained among the elect.[11]

Soon after his arrival Trapnall joined in a law partnership with John W. Cocke, his wife's brother. By 1838, the firm of Trapnall and Cocke was licensed to practice before the Arkansas Supreme Court where Daniel Ringo, Mrs. Trapnall's brother-in-law, was Chief Justice. The firm presented many cases before the Supreme Court from 1838 to 1846.[12]

In June of 1843, John W. Cocke married Mary E. Armstrong. They had one son, W. A. Cocke. This second wife died in 1847; he followed her two years later.[13] It is said that J. W. Cocke died of grief after "his beautiful young wife confessed to him on her death bed that the child whom he loved so much was not really his."[14] The law firm of Trapnall and Cocke presented its last case before the Supreme Court in 1846.

On one occasion, in 1842, Absalom Fowler collaborated on a case with Trapnall and Cocke; it was presented before the Supreme Court.

In 1839, Frederic was backed by the Labor (Mechanics) of the city for Little Rock City Alderman, although he was not elected for that position until 1844.[15]

By 1840, the Trapnalls had been in Little Rock four years. The city, with a population of 1,531, was one of the largest urban points west of the Mississippi.[16] Memphis had only 268 more people than Little Rock. Dallas,

Fort Worth, and Oklahoma City were all names of the future; Kansas City had been incorporated only a year; Houston's population was just over 1,000.[17] One reason for Little Rock's large population was the passage through it of many westward-bound settlers. The Overland Trail from St. Louis to the Southwest crossed the Arkansas River at Little Rock. Steamboat traffic had greatly increased, and there were a number of hotels on the riverfront to accommodate travelers.

Chapter VI

CHURCH

Frederic and Martha were very active in the formation of the Episcopal Church in Little Rock, just as the Trapnall family had been so instrumental in its organization in Harrodsburg. F. W. Trapnall was one of the first Vestrymen of Christ Church which the Missionary Bishop Polk had organized in 1839.[1] The members then began a building fund, to which Trapnall was a subscriber, to build their own church.[2] Construction began in the summer of 1841 at the corner of Fifth and Scott Streets. Bishop Polk donated some lots whose sale added $900 to the fund. A contract for brickwork was made with John Robbins and for carpentry with George S. Morrison, both well known builders of those days.[4]

Bishop Otey, next Missionary Bishop for the area, was sent a request signed by vestrymen of the church, including Trapnall, to consecrate their first church on November 27, 1842.[5] Accqrding to his diary, Bishop Otey reached Little Rock on November 26, "thirty-eight minutes before sundown and stopped at Mr. Trapnall's,"[6] meaning that he spent the night with the Trapnalls. He had left Cadron that morning before sunrise.[7] The next day he consecrated Christ Church.

In December, the ladies of the church, inspired by Bishop Otey's visit, undertook a money-raising project to help the church building program. They held a fair in a large hall over the market house at the foot of Main Street near the river and raised $1,106.50.[8] The ladies had planned to purchase an organ for the church with the proceeds but instead donated the entire amount to help pay debts incurred during construction. A letter was sent by the ladies "To the Wardens and Vestry of Christ Church, Little Rock" on May 20, 1843, stating their intentions, and "Trusting that you will approve of our views and accept our contribution, and that it may relieve you of embarrassment, and tend to promote the interests and prosperity of the Church."[9] A dozen names were signed individually, including Frances M. Trapnall and Mrs. Cocke. The cost of the church was recorded in the treasurer's book as $4,243.17, so their generous contribution made up nearly one-fourth of the cost of the first Episcopal Church in the state of Arkansas.[10]

Again according to Bishop Otey's diary, he visited Little Rock on Friday, February 24, 1842, and stayed the night at the Anthony House, a popular Little Rock hotel. He visited the church, and described it as "a brick edifice with organ gallery, floor laid, pews yet to be made, pulpit and the walls to be plastered, and house painted; will accomodate, when finished, 300 to 400 people."[11] After his inspection of the church building, Bishop Otey called on Mr. Trapnall and delivered a Dr. Greenfield's letter to him. He also took Mr. Trapnall's receipt for three notes left with him for collection.[12] It would appear that Trapnall also helped his church with his professional skills as a lawyer.

The church, at its completion in August 1842, is described in these words by Rev. Dr. W. P. Witsell.

> The church was in the form of a parallelogram without tower, transept, or vestry room and was built of brick. The building did not stand in the corner but was placed in the middle of the space contained in lots two, three and four. There were two aisles and two entrances from the west. The windows were made with the pointed arch pertaining to the Gothic style of architecture. In the eastern part was the chancel, as is customary with all Episcopal churches. This was enclosed with a circular railing where a pulpit placed within it was reached by a short flight of steps. The reredos, carved in walnut, also of Gothic design, was placed against the eastern wall, with the Creed and commandments inscribed on a blue background.[13]

Another source states that the church was "blue-washed for color."

> Evidently to avoid the glare of whitewash and give softness of tone, a portion of indigo or bluing was added to the lime of the mixture so that the calcimine had a light blue effect, which was not unpleasant. There were other houses in Little Rock of that time which bore the same tints, both business and residence houses.[14]

Bishop Otey also records in his diary on April 8, 1844, the confirmation of Mrs. Martha F. Trapnall.[15] Mrs. Trapnall had previously been of the Catholic faith.[16]

A tower was added later to the church under the Rectorship of Rev. A. F. Freeman.[17] On Sunday, September 28, 1873, lightening struck the bell in the tower, igniting the structure; it burned, taking all records with it.[18]

Early sketch of Christ Episcopal Church from *A History of Christ Church*

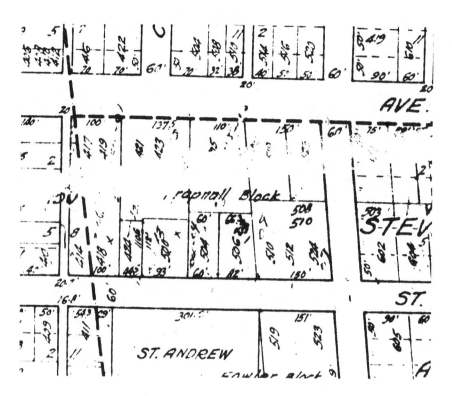

Trapnall Block in Stevenson's Addition to the City of Little Rock

Chapter VII

TRAPNALL PLACE

One of the most enduring contributions of Frederic Trapnall is his gracious home. It stands today, restored closely to its original state.

Frederic Trapnall built his family home on a gently sloping site of twelve lots which he purchased from W. W. Stevenson on June 12, 1843.[1] The lots were in the Stevenson Addition to the Original City of Little Rock. The west boundary of the land was the Quapaw Line the east boundary of the original City. The Quapaw Line bounded the land ceded to the native Quapaw Indian tribe in 1816.

The first occupants of the location chosen by Trapnall were members of the Quapaw Indian tribe, possibly of the Imbeau family, a half-Quapaw, half-French branch of the tribe.[2] But in 1824, all Quapaw lands south of the Arkansas River, including the future site of Trapnall Hall, were ceded back to the United States.

The land was included in a 1000 acre grant from the United States to the Arkansas Territory in 1833.[3] The money realized from its sale was to be used for construction of a courthouse and jail. This is thought to be part of the money that funded construction of the first state capitol.

Part of the 1000 acres was acquired by W. W. Stevenson and his wife Maria in 1835. This area was then known as Stevenson's Addition. It was from Stevenson, in 1843, that Trapnall purchased the land.[4] The oversized block purchased by Trapnall is one of only three blocks in Little Rock history that has never been given a block number. The other two are Fowler's Block and Pike's Block. Its legal description is simply "Trapnall Block." At the time Trapnall built his home, there were only a few large brick houses in the city.

Because in all legal documents of the period, as well as on the tombstones of the Trapnall family at Mount Holly, the home is called "Trapnall Place," it will be referred to as such in this paper.

First Street (now known as Commerce) came to a dead end directly in front of the Trapnall's home; Orange Street (now Fifth) ran in front of the house. Legend has it that an avenue of trees descended on either side of First Street to the river, but this seems improbable. The house rested gracefully atop a gently rising lawn. Magnolia trees grew on the grounds, and other native trees as well.[5] In Trapnall's time the grounds were probably kept by slaves, one of whom was designated a "fine gardner."[6]

There is little definite information about the actual construction of Trapnall Place or the contractor. We assume that Trapnall started construction of his home immediately after purchase of the land, for the taxable value of the land reflects improvements in 1843.[7]

Trapnall Place is built in the classic Greek Revival style that was popular throughout the country in the early 1800s. The design is similar to that of Robert Crittenden's home built several years earlier, and used as the Governor's mansion in Arkansas' territorial years.[8]

Gideon Shryock, a well-known architect from Kentucky, designed many Greek Revival structures throughout the South including Kentucky's and Arkansas' original state capitols. Although Shryock never came to Arkansas, he sent his design for her Old State House to Territorial Governor Pope. The design was too large and expensive for the young territory, so it was reduced by Pope and George Weigart. Weigart was then retained as architect for the project. Exactly what was changed from the original plans is not known, since they have been lost.

The symmetrical design of Trapnall Place can be found in Greek Revival pattern books of the period which were readily available. Although the Greek Revival influence can be felt in its design, Trapnall Place does not resemble plans of residences which Shryock is known to have designed.[9] An architectural historian of the present day, Wilson Stiles, who has studied both early Little Rock architecture and Gideon Shryock, has this to say concerning the issue.

> There has been some speculation that Shryock designed some residences in the Little Rock area, though no conclusive evidence has been found. It is interesting to note that all our early houses are not as purely Greek in form as they are Roman or carry-overs of 18th century Georgian and Federal styles. It is known that Shryock had an affinity for 18th century architecture which is evident in the few documented residences he designed in Kentucky. Perhaps he felt the Greek forms were too severe for domestic building. At any rate we have no architectural documentation on Little Rock Greek Revival residences, but it is obvious that the designers were remarkably skilled.[10]

Stiles suggests that one skilled designer in early Little Rock was R. Larrimore who advertised in the newspapers of the 1840s as an architect for residences "working in any of the five orders of architecture, either in designs or execution of the work."[11] Much of the detail work of Trapnall Place is like that found in handbooks for architects of the period, such as those written by Edward Shaw.

Construction work was later done for the Trapnalls by Little Rock builder John Wassell. He did such work for the Trapnalls as flooring a front portico, installing bannisters, handrail and columns, and sliding doors, and repairing the well house.[12] Wassell also sold lumber and other building materials to the Trapnalls. The Trapnalls had many properties to maintain and we do not know whether these services were performed on the main house, or on one of the many rental houses.

One romantic story says Frederic specified that bricks used in construction of Trapnall Place be shipped from Kentucky. This is unlikely because there were several good brick kilns in Little Rock at the time and the bricks used in Trapnall Place do not appear to be of a special type. One Little Rock kiln was run by Thomas Thorn with whom the Trapnalls later did business and who rented a place on Military Road from Mrs. Trapnall. Mrs. Trapnall had a mill on the Thorn Place.[13]

The basic plan of the house is severely symmetrical. It consists of five rooms and a wide entry hall. The hall divides the house into two equal halves; each half was divided by a sliding panelled door into two equal-sized rooms. Large double doors centered exactly on a fireplace and mantel on the opposite wall open from the hallway into each of the rooms. All of the windows and doors in the house are the same height. Trapnall Place is one of the few homes in the state in which this unique symmetry is preserved.

The front portico has four classical wooden columns. Huge panelled cypress front doors open into the fourteen foot-wide entrance hall that runs the length of the house. The hall was well suited for entertaining. An oak dining table could be extended full-length, with sixteen armchairs, eight red and eight white, arranged on either side.[14]

The Trapnalls entertained friends and business acquaintances often, and were well-equipped for such dinners. Their table settings matched the elegance of their furnishings. China and glassware owned by the Trapnalls was valued at $150 in 1863. Their silver pieces included a silver plated tea set, a silver pitcher and waiter, silver tumbers and flat silver for twelve, monogrammed M.F.T., Mrs. Trapnall's initials. The total value of the Trapnalls' silver in 1866 was $650.

Menus matched their home's appointments. Mrs. Trapnall shopped for fine foods available in Little Rock and made frequent orders for delicacies from New Orleans. When a steamer unloaded its cargo in Little Rock, merchants stocked their shelves and advertised the goods. Mrs. Trapnall's favorite grocery was Jacob Hawkin's store. There she or her servants bought cheese and crackers, various fruits - raisins, currants, apples, citron, peaches, grapes - spices such as nutmeg and cinnamon, vanilla, jellies, salad oils and brown sugar. The Trapnalls must have been fond of seafood, for she often purchased mackerel, lobster and oysters. There was a bounty of fresh meat available from the livestock they owned. Wild meat could be gotten from hunting parties. Many cigars and gallons of brandy were purchased to serve gentleman guests after dinner. Tea, whiskey and baskets of champagne were also frequent purchases. They owned a piano, and on at least two occasions hired violinists to play for their guests.

and appraisement

Inventory of Slaves and other personal property belonging or pertaining to the Estate of Fredrick R. Trapnall dec'd being a supplement to the inventory of notes made and filed, March 14, 1862, to be administered to wit.

Slaves in Pulaski County viz

1 Negro woman, named Betty, about 94 years old (childish & infirm)	no value
1 " Man, named Billy, about 84 years old, infirm	$100.00
1 " Man, named Minor, about 33 years old, delicate	800.00
1 " Man, named Lofe, about 27 years old	800.00
1 " Woman, named Betsy, about 65 years old, infirm	no value
1 " Woman, named Janetta, about 40 years old (inoculated leg)	$500.00
1 " Woman, named Amy, about 20 years old	$1000.00
1 " Boy, named Joe, about 10 years old	500.00
1 " Girl, named Matilda, about 7 years old	400.00
1 " Boy, named Phil, about 5 years old	400.00
1 " Girl, named Ophelia, about 3 years old	300.00
1 " Woman, named Angeline, about 27 years old	600.00
1 " Child a girl named Johanna, about 3 years old	300.00
1 " Infant, girl named, Cletha Telema about 1 year old	100.00
1 " Boy, named, Henry about 12 years old	700.00

Wheeled Carriages to wit

1 Fine Pleasure Carriage, nearly new (Sold to N.B. West	$600.00
1 Sett Harness for same, nearly new (Sold to N.B. West	200.00
1 Old pleasure Carriage (Sold to H. M. Rector	100.00
1 Small two horse wagon with some old gear	40.00

Horses viz

1 Pair Carriage Horses (Sold to N.B. West	$400.00
2 Mules about 12 or 13 years old	150.00

Inventory: Trapnall probate file

28

Qty	Item	Disposition	Value
1	Mahogany Canopy bed Stead	(Kept by Mrs J. M. Johnson)	$40.00
1	Common high post bed Stead	(sold at auction)	2.00
1	Sofa bed	(Kept by Mrs J. M. Johnson)	15.00
1	Walnut Lounge	(sold at auction)	5.00
1	Mahogany dressing bureau, with Glass	(Reserved for Mary R. T.)	25.00
1	do do do do	(sold to Rebecca)	15.00
1	Common old bureau	(sold to Upshur)	10.00
1	Marble Top Wash Stand	(Reserved for Mary R. T.)	10.00
1	do do do (New)	(sold at auction)	20.00
1	Rosewood Ward Robe (new)	(Kept by Mrs J. B. Johnson)	50.00
1	Mahogany do (old)	(Reserved for Mary R. T.)	40.00
1	Mahogany Commode	(Kept by Mrs J. B. Johnson)	15.00
1	Oak extension dining table	(sold by do)	50.00
1	Cherry work table	(sold at auction)	2.00
1	Side Board	(sold at auction)	40.00
1	Etagere	(Kept by Mrs J. M. Johnson)	5.00
1	Marble top side table	(sold at auction)	15.00
1	Small Sofa	(sold at auction)	25.00
2	Rocking Chairs	(sold at auction)	20.00
2	Elizabethan chairs	(Kept by Mrs J. B. Johnson)	30.00
11	Mahogany Parlor Chairs	(Reserved for Mary R. T.)	27.00
1	Musical work Stand	(do do)	25.00
1	Large Parlor Mirror	(do do)	10.00
1	Hat Rack	(Kept by Mrs J. B. Johnson)	5.00
1	Cabinet	(Reserved for Mary R. T.)	5.00
1	Piano Forte, with Cover and Stool	(sold at auction)	210.00
1	Glass Book Case	(Reserved for Mary R. T.)	25.00
1	Book case	(do do)	30.00
1	Office Chair	(sold at auction)	2.00
1	Green Split bottomed Rocking Chair	(do do)	1.50
1	Stove	(Kept by Mrs J. M. Johnson)	10.00
1	Refrigerator	(sold at auction)	15.00
1	Book Case	(Reserved for Mary R. T.)	15.00
1	Grate & fixtures	(sold at auction)	15.00
1	Parlor Stove	(Kept by Mrs J. B. Johnson)	15.00
1	Old Sofa	(sold at own Orders for J. B.)	5.00
1	Large Mahogany Bed Stead	(sold at auction)	25.00
2	Notch Tables	(do do)	50.00
1	Small dining Table	(do do)	5.00
1	Large do do	(do do)	15.00
8	Dining Arm chairs, Red	(Kept by J. Runge)	16.00
8	do do do White	(sold at auction)	12.00
2	Marble Top Pier Tables	(do do)	50.00
1	Marble Top Centre Table	(Kept by J. Runge)	25.00
2	Green Settees, Broad	(sold at auction)	10.00
2	Velvet Carpets	(Kept by Mrs J. M. Johnson)	164.00
1	Carpet	(sold at auction)	20.00
1	Old Carpet	(Reserved for Mary R. Trapnall)	5.00
1	Passage Carpet	(Kept by Mrs J. B. Johnson)	45.00
1	Velvet Hearth Rug	(do do)	15.00
1	Tapestry do do	(taken for J. R. Runge)	8.00
4	Window Cornices	(Kept by Mrs J. B. Johnson)	10.00
	Worsted Damask Curtains for Six Windows	(do do)	30.00
	Dimity Curtains for two Windows	(do do)	8.00
	White Muslin Curtains old for four Windows	(do do)	12.00
3	Feather Beds	(sold at auction)	60.00

Inventory: Trapnall probate file

New Orleans, _March 10_ 1858

Mrs. F. W. Trapnall

Bought of **DUDLEY, NELSON & CO.,**

WHOLESALE GROCERS,

Nos. 24 & 26 Common Street, and 37 & 39 Canal Street.

1 Bbl choic Sugar	244 c 8	19 52
1 D {Crush'd Sugar	96 c14	13 44
{ 1 Bag Rice	50 c5	2 50
{ 1 Bag Almons	28 c23	6 44
1 Bag Java Coffee	108 c20	21 60
1 Kitt Mess Mackrel		3 50
1 Bug Herring		75
1 Box {12 Boxs Sardins	@65	7 80
{12 Cans Oysters		6 50
{12 Drums figs	@10	15 00
{ 1 Bug fine Tea 6	c10	11 25
2 Boxs Star Candls	80 @22	17 60
½ Bbl f2 Lard oil	22 @1	24 00
1 Basket Champaign		16 00
1 Box Macaroni		4 00
1 Box 6 Botts Strawberry in jars		6 00
1 Dem 8 Golds Syrup 5 c75		4 75
Drayag		25
		180 90

Mrs. W. F. Trapnall
Care   L. Rock
Rapley & Faugert Co.   1¼% Ins° on $198   24 7/100   183 37

/s/ Jennings Bells   No Reserved Ginger to be had

Receipt: Trapnall probate file

The two west rooms of the house were probably used as bedrooms for the family and the two east rooms as parlors,[15] all luxuriously furnished. In the parlors were a parlor stove for cold weather, eleven mahogany parlor chairs, a large parlor mirror, two small sofas, a piano complete with cover and stool and a workstand to hold the music. Mary, the young daughter of the Trapnalls, born in May of 1852,[16] studied piano with Miss Alexandria Trossard. Frederic probably used a quiet corner of one parlor for his study. There he had an office chair and bookcases, but no desk.

In one bedroom, Martha and Frederic had a mahogany canopy bedstead, mahogany dressing bureau with mirror, marble top wash stand, mahogany wardrobe and mahogany commode. Another large mahogany bedstead, a high post bedstead, a sofa bed and featherbeds to warm them were available for Mary and the cousins who frequently visited the Trapnalls. One hearth was covered with a velvet hearth rug, another with a tapestry hearth rug.

A fifth room is joined to the main house by a doorway from the east rear parlor. It seems to have been an afterthought added before construction of the main house was finished. The adjoining doorway is very large and appears to have been planned as a window. The room originally had two windows on the south wall to match the two extant on the north wall. There was a small door between the two southern windows; this indicates the room may have been a family dining room with this a serving entrance to the kitchen. The original kitchen probably had a covered connection from the south porch to provide protected serving into the dining room.[17] The earliest manuscript map of Little Rock made in 1871, shows the covered hallway and attached kitchen on Trapnall Place.[18] (However, the map cannot be considered entirely trustworthy in details such as these.) A stove and "refrigerator" were included in the furnishings of the home, as well as a cherry work table.

During the 1963 restoration of the house, it was discovered that a bookcase or cupboard had once been built in on the southern side of the fireplace in this room. It had been partially removed during various remodelings. The cupboard had a low ceiling, and the brick wall above the ceiling had never been finished. Some speculate that the room may have served Frederic as a law office and study.

Originally the house had an open rear porch across the back where the family could sit in summer to enjoy the cool evening breezes.[19].

The Trapnalls had fifteen slaves in Little Rock for household chores, gardening, cooking, nursing and serving as waiting maids for the ladies. The servants drove the Trapnalls in one of the two pleasure carriages with a fine pair of horses. For work they used the two mules hitched to a wagon. In 1863, the family owned fifteen slaves, seven of whom were under thirteen and three of whom were over sixty. Their total value was $6,200. The most highly valued of them was a seventy year-old woman, Amy, who was valued at $1,000. The slaves were hired to others for special occasions or for months at a time if a neighbor needed extra help.

The large number of slaves the Trapnalls owned made it essential that out-buildings be located on the grounds. There are several references to such buildings in the probate file. The first was a hot house for which Mrs. Trapnall had windows painted and glazed in June, 1855. A general reference to "outbuildings" occurred in a petition of Daniel Ringo, administrator of the estate after the death of Mr. and Mrs. Trapnall. At one time Mrs. Trapnall purchased sixty-two yards of oil cloth carpeting, a forerunner of modern linoleum. Possibly this was for some of the other buildings on Trapnall Block, although the oil cloth was used even in fine homes, and came in a variety of designs.

The Trapnalls subscribed to *Harpers Magazine* and the *Home Journal*. They received, as well as advertised in, the *True Democrat*. The *True Democrat* of November 21, 1857, contains an ad placed by Mrs. Trapnall for a "valuable Farm for Rent."[20]

Mrs. Trapnall often ordered books from Dan Daly of 381 Broadway, New York City. A letter in the probate file concerns an edition of Shakespeare in three or four volumes that Mrs. Trapnall had asked Mr. Daly to procure for her. He replied that he could not locate one, and that the best editions came in eight to twelve volumes and cost from $18 upward according to paper, illustrations and binding. He said he would await her further directions before purchasing. The letter confirmed receipt of $199.60 from Mrs. Trapnall and discussed sending her packages of books.[21]

Mr. and Mrs. Trapnall did their evening reading by the light of candles, coal oil lamps and gaslight. Several lamps and lampwicks are listed on the inventory of the household. Gasoliers found in the attic during the 1963 restoration are thought to date back to the 1850s.

One of the first daguerrean artists to visit Arkansas, E. A. Hines, opened a studio around 1842.[22] The Trapnall family, which had previously commissioned miniatures painted on ivory, had quite a few daguerreotypes made in the early 1850s. Apparently all of these have been lost.

The Trapnalls frequently travelled. They journeyed not only to their plantation at Grand Lake in Chicot County, Arkansas, but also to visit relatives in Kentucky. The probate file contains receipts from the Galt House, a popular hotel in Louisville, Kentucky, and many tickets for steamboats. On a trip in 1855, Mrs. Trapnall was accompanied by several servants and her young cousin, Nancy Nance. Miss Nance is referred to as an adopted daughter of Mrs. Trapnall.[23] Miss Nance, age fifteen, is listed in the household of the Trapnalls on the 1850 census.[24] Apparently the young lady came from Kentucky to live with the Trapnalls. This was not unusual. Relatives often came to visit, and stayed several months. Rachael Casey, another cousin from Kentucky, also lived with the Trapnalls in the late 1850s, as did Mrs. Trapnall's nephew, W. A. Cocke, and Mr. Trapnall's brother, Philip.

From the probate file we get a more complete picture of the Trapnalls' daily activities. The Trapnalls carried a card case, well-enough considered to be repaired, rather than replaced. Gold watches are listed on

E. A. HINES,
Daguerrean Artist,

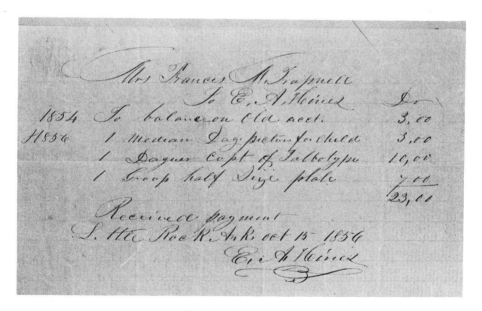

ROOM (same formerly occupied by Mr. Kellogg), upstairs in Wait's three story building, nearly opposite the Anthony House. Likenesses taken from full sized plates, down to the smallest locket, breast-pin, or ring. Work done in a fine style. Persons wishing to sit for a picture will not be charged unless the picture gives satisfaction.— Having a large instrument, of the best style, family groups can be taken with facility, and at a cost but little more than a single picture. Call and see specimens. *Nov.* 11, 1853. 27—3m.

Arkansas Gazette, November 11, 1853

Receipt: Trapnall probate file

their tax records as personal property. Mrs. Trapnall purchased gold cords and tassels to hang pictures, including a copy of the *Arkansas Traveler*. From D. C. Fulton she purchased a coral necklace, a sequined pin, two round combs and materials for dresses including merino (a fine wool), marcelaine (a thin silk used for lining vests or dresses) and a fine illusion lace. She had clothes made for her daughter Mary and bought child's gloves for Mary at Fulton's. Lastly, Mrs. Trapnall often spent thirty cents for a cake of honey soap, much kinder to a lady's complexion than homemade lye soap.

Receipts: Trapnall probate file

Chapter VIII

LAW PARTNERSHIP WITH DANIEL RINGO

Daniel Ringo, an adamant Whig, was defeated for the position of Chief Justice in 1844, and he and Frederic organized a partnership. The legal firm of Trapnall and Cocke presented only one or two cases after this time. In one, Frederic was both the defense and the accused. He was charged with stealing one of Mr. Hattier's slaves. The slave in question, never named in the suit, who had run away from Mr. Hattier, had been caught in another state and sold at auction there to a trader. The trader brought the slave to Little Rock where Trapnall bought him. Trapnall was declared innocent because he had bought the slave in good faith.[1]

Although in 1845, the Ringo and Trapnall firm brought only two cases before the Supreme Court,[2] in 1847, it brought thirty-three.[3] Other years nearly matched 1847, for sheer volume of cases the firm argued before the Supreme Court. Presumably these were not all of its cases.

In two cases, one in 1847, and one in 1850, Felix J. Batson, an attorney from Clarkesville, is listed as working on a case with Trapnall.

As Frederic's law practice grew, his legal ability, as well as his talent for public speaking, were highly acclaimed. Although Albert Pike describes Daniel Ringo as "narrow-minded, and too fond of technicalities,"[4] he says Trapnall was "in appearance, every inch a nobleman, of bright, keen, quick intellect, gracefully eloquent, whose proper place was in the halls of Congress."[5]

An incident which occurred in the court of Judge Benjamin Johnson shows us that Trapnall was not always the unruffled, southern barrister. The district attorney, William C. Scott, prosecutor, accused Trapnall, the defense lawyer, of lying. Frederic promptly knocked Scott down. Mr. Scott picked himself up, only to be fined twenty-five dollars by Judge Johnson who informed him that "when one gentleman told another that he lied, he ought to expect to be knocked down."[6]

CASES

ARGUED AND DETERMINED

IN THE

SUPREME COURT

OF THE

STATE OF ARKANSAS,

At the January Term, A. D. 1845; and of the American

Independence the sixty-ninth year.

NOTE—JUDGE LACY was not on the Bench at this Term, until within two or three days of the adjournment.

FREDERICK W. TRAPNALL, ESQ.—EX PARTE.

Upon the presentation of a proper case, this court, in the exercise of its constitutional powers, may issue a writ of *mandamus*, to a circuit court, as well as to other inferior tribunals, and enforce obedience, by attachment.

It is a prerogative writ, introduced to prevent disorder from a failure of justice and defect of police, and should be used on all occasions where the law has established no specific remedy, and justice and good government require it.

It lies to an inferior jurisdiction, or officer, to compel the performance of a duty, although a penalty is affixed by law for the nonperformance thereof.

Therefore, if a judge of the circuit court obstinately refuse to perform any duty required of him by law, this court, upon a proper showing, by the party aggrieved, would issue the writ to compel him.

To entitle a party to the benefit of the writ, he must show that he has a specific legal right, and no other legal remedy.

It may issue to compel a judge to hold a term of his court.

Acts passed upon the same subject must be taken and construed together, and made to stand if reconcilable, but to accomplish this object the obvious import of language cannot be disregarded. The intention of the Legislature must, if possible, be carried into effect, but it must be derived from the language used in the act, if it be clear and unambiguous.

Courts lean to that construction which will give effect to two acts apparently in conflict, more especially if both be passed at the same session of the legislature, but they will not suspend the operation of one act, to a future period, to give effect to another.

2

Chapter IX

CHICOT COUNTY PLANTATION AND OTHER HOLDINGS

One of Trapnall's largest holdings of land was in Chicot County.

He began to acquire this land in 1842, with J. W. Cocke. They made the high bid of $100 on land appraised at $700.[1]

Three years later, Trapnall purchased nine slaves from Catherine deVillemont in Chicot County.[2]

At various times Trapnall purchased lands that had been forfeited for non-payment of taxes including 530 acres for $98.70,[3] four acres for $4.64[4] and 160 acres for $8.19.[5]

On February 23, 1848, Ringo and Trapnall bought a large working plantation from Grandison C. Smith and his wife Ann W. Smith.[6] This plantation of 814 acres stretched from the Mississippi River to Grand Lake, with a landing on the Mississippi River to ship cotton and other produce down river to New Orleans. A cotton gin was located on the plantation.

Chicot County was reputed to have "by scientific analysis, the richest soil in the world; richer than that of the valley of the Nile."[7] In 1860, 40,968 bales of cotton were produced there.[8]

There is no mention of cotton in the inventory of the plantation at the time of purchase by Ringo and Trapnall. Probably the fall crop had been sold. There were thirty-nine slaves on the plantation, about twenty-five of whom were of an age to work in the field. The livestock included eighteen horses and mules, sixty cattle, one hundred fifty hogs and a yoke of oxen for the heaviest work. There were carts and wagons and all necessary implements of husbandry. Three thousand bushels of corn and seven thousand pounds of pork complete the inventory.[9]

Martha and Frederic spent a great deal of time at Grand Lake, perhaps using it as a country home away from Little Rock.

Trapnall also owned land in the counties of Hot Spring, Jefferson, Saline, Arkansas, Desha, Crittenden and Monroe.[10] In Jefferson County, eight hundred acres are listed as owned by Trapnall in the 1851 and 1852 tax records. The total value of these lands is listed at $4,800.[11] No information is available on the value of his lands in the other six counties.

Trapnall's most extensive land holdings were in Pulaski County. In 1840, he owned one lot in the city of Little Rock valued at $5,000. In 1841 the total value of his taxable property was $6,680. By 1848, the total value of all real estate owned by Trapnall in Pulaski County was $48,783.[12] The probate files reflect rent paid to the Trapnalls by many people for farms, warehouses, homes and rooms or offices.

Chapter X

POLITICAL BEGINNINGS

On November 14, 1843, a letter was published in the *Gazette* supporting "David Walker, of Washington, for Congress and Frederic W. Trapnall, of Pulaski for Governor."[1] The anonymous writer states that "they are both men of talents and capacity. They could do justice to the Whig party, and no men in the state could better explain the doctrines for which we battle."[2] A Whig meeting in Pope County in that same year also expressed its preference for David Walker for Congress and F. W. Trapnall for governor.[3] This is interesting support for someone who had never held political office in the state and never did run for governor.

On December 27, 1843, the Clay Club (Whig supporters of Henry Clay) met in City Hall. Two speeches were given: one by John W. Cocke who spoke although he was ill, and another by Frederic Trapnall. Trapnall's speech was described by one who was there as

> . . . one of the most argumentative and convincing harangues that we have ever had the pleasure of hearing. [Trapnall] entered fully into a discussion of the principles of the Whig and Locofoco Democratic parties of the country - he held up in its true light the conduct of self-styled democrats - showing that their principles were directly opposed to those of the founders of the government and the fathers of the revolution. He clearly proved that the Whig party were endeavoring to carry out the principles and measures on which the government was based.[4]

Trapnall also dwelt in his speech on the economic and banking problems facing the nation and state. This was a recurring theme in Trapnall's political life and a central plank in the national Whig platform.

At a Whig meeting in "Old Pulaski" held at the courthouse in early January, 1844, Trapnall was selected to run for the Arkansas House of Representatives and described as "worthy to represent any body of enlightened freemen in the Halls of Congress."[5]

Active within the party organization, Trapnall was often entrusted with the chair of committees, such as the committee to draft a "preamble and resolution expressive of the sense of the meeting"[6] and the nominating committee for governor.[7]

At a Whig convention on January 19, 1844, Frederic, as usual, was called upon to display his well-known oratorical skill. His speech was described in the *Gazette* as containing "some of the most inimitable touches that have ever fallen from his gifted mind."[8]

A Democratic newspaper, the *Arkansas Banner* also printed a less favorable review of the convention and Trapnall's speech.

> Trapnall now opened his TRAP, baited with tit bits and dainties in a very attractive manner, especially to the ladies. Frederic mounted on his stool, seemed more like a professor of Anatomy, lecturing to a class of boobies, than a politician addressing the sovereign people. He laid out upon the table a carcass which he said was once owned by a 'Loco-Foco,' and put his scalpel into it in a very summary manner! To the officers of the convention he handed the head - (they needed the *brains,* that's a fact!) - the limbs and body were distributed, in small pieces, to the class for inspection; the 'maw,' which he said was very large, he held up for the special edification of the spectators and the *ladies*! The whole audience ... testified their approbation of this delicate point with shouts and applause.[9]

Even sarcasm couldn't ignore Trapnall's appearance and popularity with the ladies.

This convention also chose Trapnall to run for the House of Representatives as the Whig candidate from Pulaski County.

During this period, Trapnall took part in uncovering a scandal connected with Samuel Trowbridge who had been elected mayor of Little Rock in a special election in May 1842. Thirteen thousand dollars in Real Estate Bank notes which had been in an iron safe in Justice of the Peace Fitzgerald's office were stolen. The bank notes were in question in a suit which Frederic had brought before Fitzgerald. Fitzgerald kept the matter quiet for some time, but he did tell Trapnall of the theft. Fitzgerald suspected Trowbridge from the start, and his suspicions were proved well-founded when Trowbridge's wife used some of the money which had been marked by Justice Fitzgerald. After the arrest, it was discovered that the mayor was involved in much more than simple theft.[10] He was found to be the mastermind of a gang of counterfeiters and burglars. The gang had been operating for about three years, specializing in making and passing counterfeit money, including gold and silver coins, bank notes of other states and corporation notes of the town of Little Rock.[11]

Trapnall was authorized by the absent Attorney General Robert W. Johnson to prosecute the case. His efforts were described as "signalized by extraordinary energy and success."[12]

Governor Yell pardoned Trowbridge after he turned State's evidence and disclosed the other members of the gang and their place and methods of operation. The Governor drew much criticism for this action from the people, who felt cheated and deceived by Trowbridge. The August 2, 1844, edition of the *Gazette* published a letter written by Trapnall supporting Yell's decision. He had been directed by Governor Yell to bargain with Trowbridge for the information. His letter, in part, reads

> I feel confident that Wilson (a co-conspirator) acted honestly; and I could not say Trowbridge did not, but there is some doubt of it in my mind. I think, however, that the Governor should grant his pardon to both, according to the agreement, as their confession and discoveries rendered a great service in finding a great many counterfeiting instruments, and in breaking up the nest of robbers and counterfeiters at Little Rock.[13]

The paper also states that Mr. Trapnall probably suffered a loss of $14,000 or $15,000 of Arkansas money which had been stolen by Trowbridge and others.

There is yet another report of a rousing political debate at which Trapnall spoke in August of 1844. His major concerns, as usual, were with the United States Bank and the tariff. Both of these were basic Whig platform issues. "The other questions of National and State policy, he handled in his usual able and felicitious manner."[14]

He spoke again at a Whig rally "giving a very beautiful speech" on October 2, 1844.[15]

Trapnall won the election and in March of 1844 he resigned as Little Rock City Alderman to accept his seat in the General Assembly as a representative to the Arkansas House from Pulaski County.[16] The fifth session of the General Assembly met in Little Rock on November 4, 1844.

Emblem from a Whig campaign banner, 1840

Chapter XI

FIFTH SESSION OF THE HOUSE OF REPRESENTATIVES

Trapnall's first official act in the fifth session was as a member of a joint committee of five appointed to wait on his excellency, Governor Adams, and to inform him that the two houses were organized and ready to receive any communication he had to send.[1] He was also on several standing committees including the Committee of Education, Committee on Internal Improvements and Committee on the Judiciary. It can be seen how active Frederic was in the House by noting some of the other committees to which he was appointed during the course of the session: a committee to elect a chaplain, a committee to investigate a petition from citizens asking for a bridge over the Arkansas River at Little Rock, the committee on Banks, a committee to study the petition of Mrs. Nancy Gaines to purchase certain real estate in her own name, a committee to define the boundary between Pulaski, Saline and Perry Counties, a committee on gaming, a committee to repeal a part of the law proscribing the power and duties of Little Rock Mayor and Alderman, numerous committees concerning the building of roads, a committee on fire hunting and a committee to consider a memorial to Congress concerning the title to the Hot Springs in Arkansas.

Trapnall made an admirable showing in the fifth session. He introduced a bill to exempt the Mount Holly Cemetery from taxation, as well as one to authorize the Secretary of State to appoint a deputy.

Two of the main concerns throughout his career were use of state monies for internal improvements, and improvement of the affairs of the State Bank. At this early date in his career, one of the amendments he presented was "an act to regulate the price and sale of the 500,000 acres of land donated to the State of Arkansas."[2] His amendment required that "the proceeds of the sale of the 500,000 acres should be applied to the payment of the State bonds and that when said bonds are purchased they shall compose the internal improvement fund."[3] This land had been given to the state by the federal government to sell, and to use the proceeds for internal improvements. Trapnall felt that the proceeds had not been used profitably.

He also sponsored a resolution commanding "that a summons be issued against the financial receivers at the Post, Batesville, and Fayetteville branches of the State Bank, to appear before the joint committee of the State Bank, on or before the 24th day of this month, to show what has become of the specie unaccounted for, and why a report has not been made on the subject as required by law." This passed fifty-five to nine.

Trapnall was on a House committee to confer with a Senate committee on the bill entitled "an act to amend an act to prohibit the emigration and settlement of free Negroes, or free persons of color, into this State," Trapnall opposed the bill. The amendment eventually met defeat because of the fear the large slave holders in the state felt for the effects of freed Negroes upon their slaves.

Trapnall presented some personal legislative bills. Legislative action was the only way a claim against the state could be collected unless it was provided for in an appropriation.

These are only a sample of the committees on which Frederic served. The Journal of the House normally reports bare facts with no descriptive terms, but the clerk made the following entry on Christmas Day, 1844.

> Mr. Trapnall rose from his seat, and in an elegant and appropriate manner asked the House to suspend all business for this day, it being a day consecrated all over the Christian and civilized world.

The motion was passed, and the House adjourned until nine o'clock the next morning.

Many letters to editors of local newspapers after this session again supported Trapnall for legislator. Early in June, the Whig convention met and organized a committee to nominate candidates for the House. Frederic stood before the committee, announced his retirement and remarked "that as he had been called upon more than once through the Organ of the party, to prevent a difficulty hereafter, he felt constrained to say that circumstances had transpired which put it entirely out of his power to become a candidate."[4] We are given no clues explaining why he refused even consideration for election - which seemed a certainty - in this year. Perhaps his growing law practice took most of his energies. This is also the period when Trapnall was soliciting construction funds for his church; this, too, may have been time-consuming.

Chapter XII

DUELS

Although dueling had been outlawed in Arkansas, as late as the mid-nineteenth century it was an accepted and even expected way for a man to defend his honor. Among other well-known duels of the period was that involving Dr. John H. Cocke, cousin to Mrs. Trapnall and an early settler in Little Rock, who had been involved in a duel early in territorial days.[1] Dr. Cocke had written some bitter denunciations of Arkansas Territorial Governor John Pope which were printed in the *Arkansas Advocate* under the penname of Dinwiddie. Major Fontaine Pope, nephew of the Governor, felt bound to defend the injury to the honor of his uncle who was old and infirm, and challenged Cocke to a duel. It took place opposite the mouth of White River in Mississippi with regulation dueling pistols at fifteen paces. Three shots were fired, but as in many accounts of duels of this period, no one was hurt. The duel was satisfactorily ended when friends of the two men interfered after the third round and the contestants allowed themselves to be talked out of continuing. Reportedly the two principals in the affair afterward became fast friends.[2]

Trapnall was apparently opposed to the needless blood-letting of duels. As a "friend" of the duelist he tried to prevent one from taking place.

In December 1843, the *Gazette* was owned by Ben Borden, a Whig and supporter of Henry Clay, Whig candidate for president. The *Arkansas Banner* was owned by Solon Borland, a Democrat. A sharp editorial bickering began between the papers. The dispute soon descended to an exchange of highly personal insults which led to a fist fight in January of 1843, when Borland thoroughly beat up Borden.[3] Friends of the two hoped this would end the matter, and six such friends went as far as to draw up and print in the two papers a statement that the difficulty had been "honorably and satisfactorily adjusted." The statement was signed by three Whigs: Frederic Trapnall, Charles Rapley and Thomas Newton, acting for Borden; and three Democrats: William Field, Lambert Reardon and Samuel Hempstead, all friends of Borland.[4]

This attempt at concilliation was unsuccessful however and a duel took place at the Indian Territory opposite Fort Smith with regulation duelling pistols at ten paces. Borden's pistol accidently went off into the ground so Borland took leisurely and deliberate aim and shot Borden in the side, wounding him badly. Although Borland regretted his actions afterward, the rivalry continued after Borden's recovery. [5]

In October of 1848, Borland received a challenge in which Trapnall had an even closer role. Thompson D. Flournoy challenged Borland to a duel as the result of allegations printed by Borland which implied Flournoy's involvement in a shady political deal. Flournoy first sent a letter by Trapnall asking Borland to recant. Borland refused, so Flournoy sent his challenge and designated Trapnall to act as his second. Borland again refused saying he had too much at stake to throw away on a senseless duel. [6]

Chapter XIII

SEVENTH SESSION OF THE HOUSE OF REPRESENTATIVES

The Seventh Session of the General Assembly convened in Little Rock on November 6, 1848.[1] Trapnall again served as a Pulaski County delegate in the House for this session. In the first meeting of the session, Trapnall was one of three men nominated for Speaker of the House. He received eighteen votes in the first ballot; no candidate received a majority. Trapnall and Izard withdrew after the first ballot to give E.A. Warren the position.

A number of contributions were made by Trapnall during this session. His most far-reaching proposal concerned the State Banks and the judiciary. He was on standing committees concerned with both of these as well as on the Education Committee. He frequently was chosen to present committee reports.

The mismanagement of the State Bank had been a political issue for several years. Trapnall introduced several resolutions requiring A. E. Thornton, financial receiver of the State Bank, to make reports to the House. He also presented a report from the Joint Committee on banking which filled fourteen pages of the House Journal. His investigations were instrumental in pointing out Thornton's inefficiency and dishonesty, and straightening out the serious problems of the Bank.

After the Governor's speech at the beginning of the session, Mr. Trapnall took it upon himself to arrange the topics suggested by the governor for consideration by the legislature and to refer them to appropriate committees. His eight resolutions to do this were all adopted.

Resolutions of a less serious nature were frequently presented by Trapnall. He presented the petition of Philip L. Anthony and others asking the legislature to incorporate the Little Rock Lyceum, an organization that provided public lectures and concerts. It was incorporated as a result of this legislation. The Lyceum considered its function to make the public aware of current trends in social entertainment, intellectual improvement and moral betterment. Meetings were held weekly at which discussion topics included phrenology, republicanism and perhaps a contemporary political issue.[2] Other community-related bills which Trapnall presented were those requesting the use of the hall of the House of Representatives by public citizens. On one occasion use of the hall was given to Rev. James Champlin who was a teacher of the blind. He used it to present a lecture on education of the blind and to illustrate his ability to train students by a public examination of one of his pupils.

Twice Trapnall requested successfully that the hall be given to the Episcopal ladies of the city to present "a vocal and instrumental concert for the use and benefit of the church."[3]

When the approval of the new county to be named Worth came before the House, Trapnall presented an amendment to the bill, proposing it be named Ashley County out of respect for Chester Ashley, an Arkansas Democratic senator who had died. Earlier in the session "after some eloquent and appropriate remarks" by Trapnall, a resolution had been adopted concerning Ashley's death and expressing the regret of the members of the legislature.

Trapnall presented a petition filed by his wife's brother John W. Cocke as executor of the will of John Pope, late governor of the Arkansas Territory, concerning debts owed by Pope to the state. The debts were eventually forgiven owing to the services rendered the state by Pope.

Once when Trapnall moved to refer some proposed amendments to the constitution to a committee of the whole, he was told by the Speaker of the House that his motion was out of order. He appealed to members of the house to back him up, but was overruled. When the amendments came up for vote, Trapnall's stubborn "No" vote was the only one cast in several cases.

Trapnall also introduced a bill to incorporate the South Western and Arkansas Mining Company, and a bill to lessen the printing expenses of the government.

Trapnall was still concerned with the use of the 500,000 acres donated by the United States Government to the state of Arkansas and was appointed to a select committee for deciding the specific use of the funds. He proposed a strict act to track the monies. He attempted to amend a bill that supported buying bonds with the money but the bill passed without his amendment. Eventually the money was squandered without substantial returns for the state.

Chapter XIV
PHILIP TRAPNALL

At about this time, Frederic's youngest brother, Philip, arrived in Little Rock. Philip was born in 1827, just two years before Frederic moved away from his family to practice law in Springfield.

Philip received the A.B. degree from Bacon College at Harrodsburg in 1847.[1] Very soon after his graduation, he left for Arkansas following in the footsteps of his older brother. Although the time of his arrival cannot be determined exactly, he was involved in the Whig organization for young men, the Rough and Ready Club, in Little Rock by July 24, 1848.[2] Also in 1848, although he was only twenty-one years old, Philip was licensed to practice law before the Arkansas Supreme Court.[3]

The law partnership between Trapnall and Ringo had dissolved around 1848, when Ringo was appointed by President Taylor to fill the position of Judge for the United States District Court, District of Arkansas, that was created at the Hon. Ben Johnson's death.

Philip lived with his brother during his first few years in Little Rock. By 1851, Philip and Frederic had formed a law firm of their own in which Philip was the junior partner. The brothers handled many cases in 1851 and 1852.[4] Philip proved to be a brilliant lawyer and learned quickly from his experienced brother.

3 o'clock, P. M., Jan'y 6, 1851.

The House convened.

Mr Trapnall from the committee on the judiciary to whom was referred House bill 241 to be entitled an act to regulate steamboats in the discharge and delivery of freight on the Arkansas river, reported the same back to the House favorably.

On motion of Mr James the rules were dispensed with and the bill was read a third time and passed.

Mr Trapnall from the committee on the judiciary to whom was referred House bill 224 to be entitled an act to define the privilege of persons who may have had license to hawk and peddle without license, reported the same back to the House with sundry amendments, and recommended its passage.

Which report was adopted and the rules were suspended.

On motion of Mr. Johnson, the bill was read a third time and passed.

Mr Trapnall from the committee on the judiciary to whom was referred House bill 237 to be entitled an act amending an act establishing justices of peace courts, reported the same back to the House and recommended its rejection.

Which report was adopted and the bill rejected.

Mr. Trapnall from the committee on the judicary to whom was referred House bill 185 to be entitled an act to change the forms of pleading in the circuit courts, reported the same back to the House with an amendment and recommended its passage.

Which report was adopted.

On motion of Mr. Tappan the rules were dispensed with and the bill was read a 3d time and passed.

Chapter XV

EIGHTH SESSION OF THE HOUSE

The Eighth Session of the House of Representatives began on November 4, 1850, and for the last time, Frederic Trapnall represented Pulaski County at the session.[1] As in the seventh session, he was nominated for Speaker of the House. He received sixteen votes on the first ballot, but none of the three nominees received a majority. The voting went on through eleven ballots before Flournoy, a good friend of Trapnall, was elected. Through all these votes Trapnall never voted for himself, but courteously gave his support to Flournoy. Trapnall's supporters took a long time to be persuaded to change their votes. Even as late as the eighth ballot, Trapnall had fourteen votes.

In this session Trapnall was chairman of the judiciary committee, and served on standing committees concerning apportionments and public printing and on the important committee on federal relations. He was also on numerous appointed committees.

The State Bank scandal was resolved during this session. A. E. Thornton, mainly as a result of Trapnall's thorough investigations, was labeled a defaulter considered guilty of "forgery, embezzlement and other crimes by which the bank had been defrauded out of large sums of money." Thornton escaped his just punishment by fleeing the state and was last reported in Mexico.

Many bills introduced by Trapnall, or recommended favorably by his committees, concerned internal improvements. There were bills concerning a turnpike through the Ouachita Swamp, a ferry across the Ouachita River, a toll bridge across Bayou de Roche, the construction of levies, drainage, and the establishment of poor houses. He presented a substitute for a bill concerning the House chaplains, which created the office of Chaplain of the House. Although he was not a Mason, he introduced a bill to incorporate the trustees of the Little Rock Masonic and Odd Fellows Hall.

Trapnall's judiciary committee recommended rejection of a bill which would give justices of the peace jurisdiction over the crime of Sabbath-breaking. The bill was rejected as recommended.

Trapnall introduced one bill to amend the State Constitution to provide for public election of the Secretary of State, State Auditor, State Treasurer, County judges and judges of the Supreme Court. The bill was defeated. Trapnall was about a decade before his time, for his suggestions became law in 1864. He also sought to create the state office of geologist, but was defeated.

In the Eighth General Assembly serious questions began to arise concerning salvery and states' rights. Trapnall took a very active part in these discussions.

One of his first actions was recommendation of a bill to amend the Statutes of the State concerning free Negroes and mulattoes. He then recommended the rejection of a bill to "prohibit persons from quartering slaves on plantations or other places without overseers." Trapnall was also very active in drafting a bill concerned with the treatment of slaves.

Trapnall served on the Joint Committee on Federal Relations to which was referred a part of the governor's message given at the beginning of the session. The section of the message related to federal acts and policy. The report issued by the chairman of the committee, George Eaton, claimed the Federal Government had

> ... increased in strength and grown with each successive year, until it has absorbed all power, and clothed itself in colors more glowing than had ever been painted in fancy or dream.
>
> Thus the Federal Government commencing its career as a joint commission on the part of thirteen sovereignties, has extended its influence, step by step, until its feet are placed upon the necks of the prostrate States, bestriding the Continent, and rearing a front more imposing than Imperial Rome, or that Mistress of the Seas, upon whose extended domain the sun never sets.

The report had other harsh criticisms of the federal government, especially of its actions in Mexico and California; it called these actions a "spirit of aggression upon Southern rights," and said, "the bold and reckless assumption of power by the Federal Government in the premises aforesaid, are alarming, dangerous and perilous to the slave holding states."

The joint committee made clear its ideas on slavery.

> The domestic institution of African slavery as it now exists in the Southern States is worthy of extension and perpetuity, and affords a happy facility for the moral elevation of both the black and white races, and is fully sanctioned by divine law.

Immediately after the presentation of the report, Trapnall moved to lay the report and resolution on the table indefinitely. The vote was forty-one to twenty-eight in favor of Trapnall's motion.

The following joint resolution of the Senate was read on motion of Trapnall.

Resolved, by the General Assembly of the State of Arkansas, That our warm and cordial approbation be, and the same is hereby extended to our delegation in Congress for all that part of their public and official conduct, which had for its object the sustenance of the rights of the South against the aggressive legislation and spirit of the late Congress of the United States.

This was worded entirely too gently for some of the members of the Senate. Mr. Tebbets offered the following as a substitute.

We condemn all action of the people of the non-slave holding States, and their representatives in Congress affecting prejudicially the rights or interests of the Southern States on the subject of slavery.

We still, not withstanding all the wrongs we have suffered at the hands of our northern brethren, adhere to the Union of the States. But we solemnly protest against a further interference with our Constitutional rights on the subject of slavery with a fixed determination to resist further aggression by all legal and Constitutional means - and if necessary to resort to such other means as are guaranteed to freemen by the laws of nature and nature's God.

Again Trapnall moved to lay both the resolution and the substitute on the table indefinitely. He was backed forty-three to twenty-two. It would seem that although the problem was real and was recognized by the Representatives, they were not ready to grapple with the realities it presented.

The Eighth Session of the General Assembly adjourned on January 13, 1851.

Sally Faulkner (left), Annie Merrick: Courtesy of J. N. Heiskell Library of the Arkansas Gazette Foundation

Chapter XVI

FAMILY STORIES

A happy event occurred in the Trapnall family in the Spring of 1851; Philip married Sallie Faulkner.[1] The ceremony, which took place at the home of the Faulkners on April 29, was performed by Rev. Andrew Freeman, rector of Christ Episcopal Church.[2]

Sallie was the daughter of Col. Sanford Faulkner, the originator of the Arkansas Traveler story. She was known for her beauty and sought-after by the young men of the city.

Philip had been successful at his law practice so the couple was not wanting for material wealth. Philip was well respected throughout the city, as is shown by his election as city alderman the following year.[3] The couple probably made their home on twelve lots owned by Philip located northwest of the Old State House. Philip owned considerable land in Little Rock as well as farm property in Pulaski County.[4]

Their home was amply furnished.[5] There were Brussels carpets on the floors and mahogany and walnut furniture throughout. Philip had a mahogany bookcase to contain the law library inherited from his father; he entertained his clients and friends in a well-stocked dining room. The couple owned four slaves, a carriage and various livestock.

Philip possessed one of the family heirlooms, a gold watch valued at $40 in his inventory and seals that had been left to him by his Uncle Henry Trapnall.

Unfortunately Philip's time in Little Rock was short; five years after his marriage he died. The *True Democrat* reported his death.

> Died at his residence in this city on the 2nd instant, Mr. Philip Trapnall. The deceased was a native of Kentucky, but emigrated to this State several years since. He was by profession a lawyer and with talents of superior order and a mind well stored with information, his prospects for winning distinction in the profession he had chosen were unusually bright.
>
> Distinguished alike for his real excellence of heart and many manly virtues, he had gone to the grave amid the heartfelt regrets of a numerous circle of friends.[6]

Philip's will was very concise: "To my beloved and cherished wife, Sallie, I bequeath all of my estate, real, personal, and mixed." It was written on what appears to be a folded embossed piece of stationary and dated December 19, 1854.[7] The will does not appear to be in Philip's handwriting.

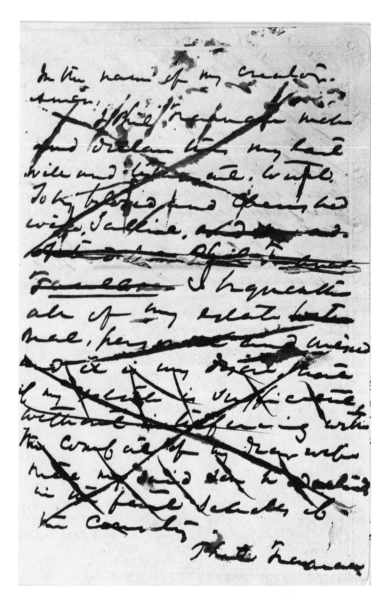

Will as found in Philip Trapnall probate file

Within a short two years after the death of Philip, his entire estate had been liquidated by Sallie, who assessed nothing in 1857.[8] She then moved in with her aging father, Sanford Faulkner. Philip and Sallie had no children, but she did have a nephew named Philip Trapnall after her husband.

The *Arkansas Gazette* of March 5, 1880, printed a story about Sallie that came from the Louisville *Courier-Journal*. It was titled "No Longer A Belle: The Sad Story of 'The Most Beautiful Woman in Arkansas.' "The story reads that "her wardrobe came from Paris and her lovers from everywhere. Slave to the demands of gaiety and conquest she was haughty and considered heartless. Her sway for years was undisputed and when her financial decline came she would not recognize a fact which seemed to her so preposterous." The story then states that Sallie's circle of friends was planning a trip to New Orleans for the Mardi Gras. Sallie bemoaned the fact that she could not afford to go with them. Major Henry M. Brown heard Sallie and made a proposal - he would take her to New Orleans if she would marry him. Sallie gaily agreed.[9] The marriage was performed February 5, 1860, and the trip to New Orleans took place.[10] It is important to remember that this story was told by one who met Sallie in later years, and who did not know her well. Many of the facts in the story were wrong. Margaret Ross, who has studied the life of Sallie Faulkner Trapnall intensively, states in reference to the article, that "although the facts were brutally garbled, the article is probably a more or less accurate index to the malicious gossip that went the rounds of the jealous women and spurned men."[11]

Sallie was not fated for a happy life. The marriage with Major Brown was not successful and she spent the remainder of her years with her father. She is listed in the 1860 census soon after the wedding as living in her father's home, without her husband. She was known for the rest of her years as Mrs. Trapnall. After her father's death in 1874, she lived alone except for the niece she reared who was the daughter of her dead sister Mattie. Sallie was involved in a buggy accident and as a result lost a leg. She died October 30, 1881, poor and begging on the streets of Little Rock.[12]

On May 7, 1852, at Trapnall Place, a daughter, Mary Ringo, was born to Frederic and Martha Trapnall.[13] She was named for Mrs. Trapnall's sister, Mary Cocke Ringo.

The New York *Spirit of the Times*, mentions Trapnall in a story in the "Arkansiana, etc." column in 1852. The title of the story is "Financially Your Friend."

> Poor old Will Triplett! He killed a man in Little Rock, in a fit of temporary insanity, produced by drinking, a civil officer who was arresting someone when Triplett pitched into the fight, without cause or provocation, and cut down the officer with a Bowie knife. He was committed to jail, and died there of a broken heart, before his trial came on.

He was once a witness in a case where a man had shot another. Fred Trapnall was counsel for the prisoner.

"Now Triplett,' said he, "did the prisoner exhibit any malice prepense, any ill will towards the deceased previous to shooting him?"

"I don't know," said Triplett, "what you mean by malice prepense, but it seems to me he loaded his pistol with a great deal of *elasticity*."

Soon afterwards Trapnall was elected to the legislature. Triplett had always been in the habit, whenever he was out of money, an event of no rare occurrence, of going to Trapnall to borrow - an undertaking in which he always succeeded - though Trapnall was a Whig and he a Democrat.

When the legislature met, Triplett announced himself a candidate for doorkeeper of the House, and went to Trapnall to engage his vote.

"See here, Triplett," said Trapnall, "you are always running to me to borrow money, and now you want my vote for doorkeeper, and yet whenever I am a candidate you are sure to vote against me in favor of every Democrat that runs."

"Trapnall," said Triplett with grave earnestness, "politically I am your enemy, but *financially* I have always been your friend."[14]

This story became well-known in Arkansas. It was referred to in the *Arkansas Gazette* in an article about the reopening of the *Arkansas Whig* newspaper. The *Gazette* editor wished the new owners of the paper, Stillwell and Wassel, good luck and quoted, "As Bill Triplett said to Trapnall *financially* we are with him but *politically* we are opposed to him."[15]

Chapter XVII

THE CAMPAIGN FOR CONGRESS

In Camden on May 12, 1853, the State Whig Convention showed the extreme respect and high regard in which they held Frederic Trapnall by unanimously nominating him as the Whig candidate for Congress.[1] He was to campaign to represent the newly created Southern District of Arkansas which, established after the 1850 census, reflected the rapid growth of the state. The *Arkansas Whig* printed a letter from an anonymous person with the penname A.U.R.E.L.I.U.S., who predicted "such a political battle as was never fought in this state."[2] He describes Trapnall as "one of the first political debators in any country. Trapnall carves up his opponents in an intellectual conflict, with such keen blade, that they never know they are hurt until just before they faint."[3] Trapnall's Democratic opponent, Col. E. A. Warren, from Ouachita County, was also well-known for his ability in debate. Of him, A.U.R.E.L.I.U.S. said, "Warren speaks like putting out fire, is never at a loss for facts, and throws his logic about in great lumps."[4]

At this juncture newspapers began to refer to Trapnall as Colonel Trapnall. Though no justification for the title has been found, people who have since lived in Trapnall's home tell stories of "Colonel" Trapnall.

The same newspaper printed a letter from Frederic accepting the nomination. It is one of the few documents we have that was written by Trapnall.

In it Trapnall cheerfully accepted the nomination and set out the issues of the campaign. He stated, "I shall enter the campaign with a strong and willing heart; and everything which dilligence, energy, and zeal can accomplish for our glorious cause, shall be fully performed by me in carrying out its wishes."[5] Then he attacked the ills of "Abolitionism, Free-solism, the rampant spirit of Fillibusterism, Nullification, and the spirit of Repudiation," and glorified "the temperate and conservative influence of Whig principles and the ascendancy of Whig counsels."[6]

Other than strongly-worded criticisms of the Democratic Party, the two main issues he addressed were major Whig tenets; the use of public lands to assure internal improvements, and the building of railroads. He criticized the Democrats for not taking action on both issues. The public lands that the federal government had granted to Arkansas were to be used for internal improvements. Trapnall felt that the present state government had not made good use of the money from the lands.[7]

GAZETTE & DEMOCRAT.

LITTLE ROCK.

FRIDAY MORNING, JUNE 24, 1853.

☞CIRCULATION☜

Larger than any other Paper in the State.
OFFICE, UP STAIRS, IN BEEBE'S BUILDINGS,
ON MARKHAM AND ELM STREETS.

Democratic Nominations for Congress.

FIRST DISTRICT,

A. B. GREENWOOD,

OF BENTON COUNTY.

SECOND DISTRICT,

E. A. WARREN,

OF OUACHITA COUNTY.
Election to be holden on the first Monday of August, 1853.

Public Speaking.

E. A. WARREN, candidate for Congress in the Southern District of Arkansas, will address his fellow-citizens at the following times and places:

Saturday	25th of June,	Lawrenceville, Monroe co.	
Monday	27 " "	Brownsville, Prairie	"
Thursday	30 " "	Pine Bluff, Jefferson	"
Saturday	2 " July,	Little Rock, Pulaski	"
Monday	4 " "	Benton, Saline	"
Wedne'y	6 " "	Perryville, Perry	"
Friday	8 " "	Danville, Yell	"
Monday	11 " "	Waldron, Scott	"
Wedne'y	13 " "	Fort Smith, Sebastian	"
Friday	15 " "	Dallas, Pope	"
Saturday	16 " "	Mt. Ida, Montgomery	"
Monday	18 " "	Rockport, Hot Spring	"
Tuesday	19 " "	Princeton, Dallas	"
Wedne'y	20 " "	Arkadelphia, Clark	"
Thursday	21 " "	Murfreesboro, Pike	"
Saturday	23 " "	Paraclifta, Sevier	"
Monday	25 " "	Washington Hempstead	"
Wedne'y	27 " "	Lewisville, Lafayette	"
Thursday	28 " "	Strange's, Columbia	"
Saturday	30 " "	Camden, Ouachita	"

Speaking to begin at 10 o'clock A. M. of each day. Papers in the District please copy.

I should be happy to meet Hon. F. W. Trapnall, the *whig* candidate for said District, at the above named times and places.

E. A. WARREN.

☞Col. F. W. TRAPNALL, the whig candidate for Congress, has accepted the above invitation and agreed to meet Col. WARREN at all of his appointments.

Arkansas Gazette and Democrat, June 24, 1853

These years were the initial period of growth for the railroad industry. Trapnall was enthusiastic in his support of the railroad and critical of the Democratic view. In the letter, he said, "instead of eagerly seizing this bright prospect of redeeming our State from its isolation, and bringing our people in connection with the business and trade of the world, our Government stands stupidly gazing on."[8] Trapnall's opponent supported building "good dirt roads" instead of leaping ahead to railroads for which he felt the state wasn't ready.[9] Trapnall had had earlier experience testing a railroad engine when he was in Springfield, and although this first-hand experience had been an unpleasant one, he was strongly convinced of the benefits to be gained by railroad travel.[10]

He was one of the first members of the Board of Directors of the Arkansas Central Railroad Company. This corporation's goal was to build a railroad from "the western bank of the Mississippi River, opposite Memphis, to the city of Little Rock."[11] In the summer of 1852, soon after the formation of the company, Trapnall frequently made speeches to the legislature in an effort to raise money for construction of the railroad.[12] Again Trapnall proves to be ahead of his time; railroads later proved to be important to the development of Arkansas.

The *Arkansas Gazette* announced Col. Trapnall's nomination for Congressional candiate with a touch of wry humor.

> Col. F. W. Trapnall has been nominated by the Whig convention at Camden, as the candidate of the Whig party for Congress. He is a gentleman of fine talents and attainments, and one of the best Whig orators in the state. As the decree has gone forth that a Democrat has to be elected and a Whig beaten, we know of no gentleman in the Whig party who can submit more gracefully to a defeat than can Col. Trapnall. It may be that his peculiar qualification in this respect has been the reason of his choice by the Camden convention.[13]

The two candidates immediately began a canvass of the second district. Their travel schedule was printed in the newspaper so all were aware of where and when their debates would be held.[14] By the second of June, Col. Trapnall had returned from a campaign tour through Perry, Yell, Scott and Sebastian counties. The *Gazette* had favorable things to say about the general disposition of the voting public in these counties to change the old order, and turn to the Whigs.[15] Political observers gave Trapnall the advantage in the campaign because he was well-known all over the state, especially in southern Arkansas where his large plantation was located. Col. Warren was not very well-known outside his home county of Ouachita. The *True Democrat* voiced its worries. "In the Southern District we have a witty and cunning foe. Frederic Trapnall is a fine speaker. . .can we resist him! That is the question."[16]

The Democratic opposition had its criticisms to make of Frederic's legislative career. Their first full-scale attack appeared in the *Gazette* of June 10, 1853, in an article entitled "Look to the Record."

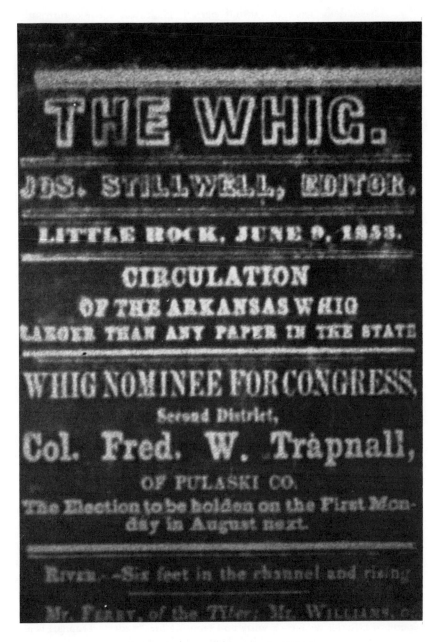

The Arkansas Whig, June 9, 1853

Our friend of the Whig, in animadverting upon Col. Warren's legislative career, seems to forget that his friend and favorite Col. Trapnall has also been a member of our State Legislature every season from 1840 to 1850, a term of ten years. During this time, a man of Col. T.'s ability has had ample opportunities to erect a monument to his legislative fame, as unperishing as marble. But for that monument we have looked in vain. If Col. Trapnall has left any record of his career in our State Legislature by which his name should stand higher on the roll of legislative fame than any of his fellow legislators, it has never come to our knowledge.

So far as our memory serves us, Col. Trapnall has distinguished himself in our legislature only as a grumbler. This has been his course and policy, fault-finding and abuse has been the burden of his song. Whilst he has been lavish in his condemnation of the course of others, he has not if we remember aright, brought forward any great measure of public policy, calculated to redound to the benefit of the State, and the credit of his name.

In this brief notice, however, we write from memory, but we do not think we can be far wrong. Next week we propose looking into the legislative career of Col. Trapnall and if he has done anything to deserve it, we will erect for him a pyramid of his legislative acts - that he and the people may have the benefit of them.[17]

The author's basic facts were wrong, as the supporters of Trapnall rushed to point out. The *Arkansas Whig* of June 16, 1853, repudiated the attack.

Our friend of the *Gazette and Democrat* . . . is wide of the mark at the outset; Col. Trapnall was not a member of the legislature from 1840-1850. He was not a member in 1840, 1842, or 1846; but he was a member in 1844, 1848, and 1850, and had he been in an assembly composed of men who listened to the voice of reason, or were actuated by motives other than that of public plunder, he might have erected that monument.[18]

Both articles should be viewed purely as political propaganda.

The next week, the article promised by the *Gazette* writer was published. This time criticism was heaped on Trapnall for his presentation of "acts for the relief of F. W. Trapnall." The article implies that he had been unethical in presenting such a bill while he was a member of the body granting the relief, that Trapnall had perhaps confused the benefit of himself with the benefit of the people and that many of the bills he did get through in his career were of the private character just described.[19]

The legislation referred to was House Bill Number 147, passed by the Seventh General Assembly. It was a claim made by Trapnall for his services as attorney on behalf of the state in various cases. The committee which was appointed to investigate the claim reported favorably.

> The committee to whom was referred an act for the relief of F. W. Trapnall for services as attorney on behalf of the State in cases referred to in said act beg leave to report that in their opinion, a reasonable compensation should be allowed and beg leave to report favorably to the bill, all of which is respectfully submitted. [20]

The bill passed forty-two to nineteen. Some of those who voted negatively may have been political opponents of Trapnall, or lawyers who were resentful that Trapnall had been appointed attorney by the state in these cases. They may have felt that his fee was too high or that the work had not been satisfactory or properly authorized. We do not know the basis for their objections, or if these objections were valid. However, only one such act was ever presented for the relief of Frederic Trapnall. The act had also passed in the Democratic Senate and had been signed by Governor Drew, a Democrat.

> *An Act For the Relief of F. W. Trapnall*
> Be it enacted by the General Assembly of the State of Arkansas, that the sum of five hundred dollars be and the same is hereby appropriated to pay F. W. Trapnall, for services rendered as attorney to the State in sundry cases, out of money in the Treasury not otherwise appropriated. [21]

There were various other articles critical of both Trapnall and his opponent written in the heat of the campaign.

> The periodic reports in the *Arkansas Whig,* the *Camden Herald,* and other Whig newspapers on the progress of the campaign cast favorable light on Trapnall's bid for Congress. On June 16, 1853, the *Arkansas Whig* reports, "Col. F. W. Trapnall . . . was in Camden on Saturday morning and left for El Dorado. Appears to be in fine health and spirits and looks and feels very much like a man who was destined to a seat in the halls of Congress next winter." [22]

Chapter XVIII

THE DEATH OF FREDERIC W. TRAPNALL

On July 1, 1853, Trapnall, at Monticello for a speaking engagement with his opponent Col. Warren, was suddenly confined with a "severe attack of sickness."[1] We have no clues to the specific nature of this illness. Mrs. Trapnall, Philip, and the family physician, Dr. A. Watkins, left by steamboat on the night of July 1, to attend to Trapnall.[2] Col. Warren did not keep the speaking engagement, but simply made a short appearance, spoke of the illness of his competitor and retired out of respect for Trapnall.[3] He announced that he did not intend to continue the canvass until Col. Trapnall recovered.[4] Anxious friends in Little Rock received favorable accounts as Trapnall began to improve, and the Doctor said he was no longer in danger of death.[5]

But on the early morning of July Fourth, Trapnall began to fail. He prayed the Lord's Prayer, gave a blessing on his wife and child, and died at five in the morning.[6]

Two days later the steamer "Col Drennen" brought the body of Frederic home to Little Rock. The steamer approached the wharf where many friends of the family waited, with bells tolling the dire news and its flag at half mast.[7]

Funeral services were conducted on July 8 by Rev. Freeman.[8] A large number of the citizens of the city attended. The coffin was draped in black cloth with black ribbon rosettes and silver tacks adorning it.[9] A horse-drawn hearse carried Trapnall to his final resting place in Mount Holly Cemetery.

Tributes of respect and expressions of regret were forthcoming from almost every newspaper in the state.

> *True Democrat:*
> For ourselves we scarcely know how to approach the subject of Mr. Trapnall's probable death. Knowing him as we have since our boyhood - so full of talents and graces that become a man, so rich in joyousness of temper, we cannot realize the fact that he is no more to us forever.[10]

Danley, editor of the *Arkansas Gazette* respectfully reversed the column rules bordering the column containing Frederic's obituary:

> A shade of gloom was cast over our city last Wednesday night by the intelligence flying with electric rapidity that Col. Frederic W. Trapnall was dead.
>
> The arrival of the boat was looked forward to by all with rejoicing because we had been informed that Col. Trapnall was convalescing and with his devoted wife, brother, and friends would then probably return home, with renewed health, and rebuoyed spirits; and again take the place so long and so well filled by him in our community, as one of our best citizens, ablest lawyers, most accomplished gentleman, most public spirited man, and last, but best, most devoted in his affections to his family and friends.
>
> But alas! human hopes are as evanescent as the clouds and sunshines of April - as delusive as the *mirage*! Instead, as we had hoped, of meeting our friend restored to health - the sparkling of his eyes, and the music of his voice, shedding a halo of joy and gladness everywhere, among his friends as was their wont, nothing returned but his cold corpse, laid low, by the hand of death. His spirit had winged its way to God who gave it; and the weeping friends could only pay their last sad tribute to his mortal body.[11]

The Wardens and Vestrymen of Christ Church, the church Trapnall had been so instrumental in erecting, expressed their feelings in a preamble and resolutions unanimously adopted on July 8, 1853.

> Whereas, Almighty God, in his wise providence, has seen fit to take out of this world the soul of our late brother and fellow-vestryman, Frederic W. Trapnall; therefore be it,
>
> Resolved, That we recognized in Mr. Trapnall an active, enterprizing, and liberal member of the congregation of Christ Church and of this vestry; and that, in submission to the Divine will, we mourn his death, as a calamity to the Prostestant Episcopal Church in this city.
>
> Resolved, That feeling acutely our own loss in being deprived of the valuable counsel and substantial encouragement of the deceased in the work of the church, we offer our deepest sympathy to his widow and relatives.
>
> Resolved, That in token of respect for the memory of the deceased we will wear the usual badge of mourning for thirty days.
>
> Resolved, That a copy of these resolutions, signed by the Rector, Wardens and Vestry, be sent to the family of the deceased.[12]

The County Court of Jefferson County and all members of the bar of that county also expressed their regret in legal proceedings in a meeting on July 5, 1853.[13]

When the Supreme Court met, on Friday, July 8, 1853, Attorney General Clendenin addressed the court in respect to Trapnall's death.

> The deceased, who was a native of Kentucky, emigrated to Arkansas in the fall of 1836, and commenced the practice of the law in this city, where he early took that eminent stand in his profession which he continued to retain until his death. Gifted with great eloquence, he ranked among the foremost advocates of the State - profoundly versed in his profession, he was well calculated to advise and counsel those who sought his services - of a most kind heart and winning manners, with a graceful and courtly address, he won the regard not only of those associated with him in this profession, but of all whom business or pleasure brought in his way.[14]

The Bar Association in which Trapnall had served for seventeen years expressed its respect and deep grief in his death in a series of resolutions. After the resolutions were passed, Albert Pike rose and said:

> "May it please your Honors: Frederic W. Trapnall, for nearly seventeen years a leading and eminent member of the bar of this Court, died at Monticello, in Drew County, in this state on Monday last, at 5 o'clock in the morning, after a painful illness of a very few days.
>
> After we had been distressed with the information of his dangerous illness, we were encouraged, from favorable accounts sent to us, to hope that he had commenced to improve, was not in danger of death, and would soon be among us to gladden us with his genial presence; and I am sure that when that cheering news arrived here, there was no one among us who did not feel that he had not until then been conscious how much he regarded, admired and loved the friend, the sudden news of whose loss soon after struck so sharp a blow upon the hearts of the community . . .
>
> There are none of us who have not felt the genial influences of his cheerful, frank and manly temper and disposition; who have not admired the grace and eminent courtesy of his manners and the vigor and quickness of his intellect. Amply armed with all the resources of the advocate, he was seldom found unprepared, or taken by surprise. Zealous in behalf of his clients, skillful and forcible in attack, and prompt and efficient in defence, he brought to the aid of his large supply of legal learning, a profound and instinctive sense of right, and a forcible, sparkling and pursuasive eloquence. Nature had been eminently liberal to him, and he had not been ungrateful to her for her bounty, but had cultivated well his ripened intellect by an extensive and judicious course of

reading. In the social circle, he charmed every one. Few men excelled him in conversational power; none in the grace and elegance of his deportment. He was formed to charm men and women alike; and in any forum, in any legislative body, in any assembly of frank and fashion, he would have been a noted and distinguished man.

His memory will not die for many years among us. We shall long, very long, miss him in our daily walks, fancy we hear the cheerful tones of his voice, and look in vain for his pleasant and seemly countenance ... And I declare that, in all my intercourse with him during so many years, I never knew the slightest approach on his part towards any thing not perfectly frank, manly, and honorable ...

That he had faults, is to say he was a man and liable to err; that he had enemies, is to say he was one of the few who achieved enviable distinction. Such a man could not fail to attach to himself many ardent friends. Eminent for his talents, but not exalted by official station, he was, in a republic, one of its great commoners.[15]

Another summation of the career of Frederic Trapnall was written in 1903 by George Rose which provides insight into how this century's lawyers think of Trapnall.

Frederick W. Trapnall, the pride and favorite of the bar presented to Fowler a striking contrast. He was the beau-ideal of the perfect gentleman, with the dignified courtly manners of the old school. As a lawyer, he was perhaps Fowler's equal, though his mind was concerned rather with great principles than with points of practice; and he sought rather to persuade than to drive. And for persuasion he was admirably fitted. He was truly a silver-tongued orator, distinguished for the refined elegance of his diction, and it was hard to resist the appeal of one so handsome, so eloquent, so kindly, and so urbane.

He was as fond of congenial companionship as Fowler was lonely, and all agree that his conversation was brilliant and entertaining to an extraordinary degree. In every social circle he was the centre of attraction for men and women alike. Always tactful and considerate of others, he guided the conversation into pleasant channels, and was beloved of all ...

His death was universally lamented. It was felt that the Bar had lost its brightest ornament and each good man a friend.[16]

James M. Curran took the nomination for Senator after Trapnall's death. The canvass was not continued out of respect to Trapnall.[17] Curran lost to Colonel Warren.

Chapter XIX

MARTHA FRANCIS TRAPNALL

Mrs. Trapnall lived for eight years after the death of her husband. She raised her one-year-old daughter and several cousins as well. Her home continued to be a center of social life in Little Rock.

In his will, Frederic bequeathed all his property to his wife. He stated " . . . and having the most implicit confidence in her prudence and discretion, this device is unaccompanied by any qualification or advice."[1] Also in the will, Frederic says, "I regret only that it is to take effect by a departure from all I hold dear and that it is so small an evidence of my affection."[2] The estate was valued at about $100,000 at Frederic's death.

The last request made by Trapnall in his will is that his executor, John Watkins Cocke, "see that every cent I owe, to whomsoever it may be due, is paid, that no one, may have any complaint to make of me."[3] John W. Cocke had died before Trapnall, so Daniel Ringo was appointed executor.

Mrs. Trapnall had moved into a new territory with her new husband at the age of sixteen and had soon become mistress of one of the larger homes in the area. As a young mother she lived through the grief of losing her first-born son, and remained a gracious hostess for her prominent husband. She became one of the foremost hostesses of the city and acquired an aptitude for her husband's business. After the death of her husband when their only living child was a year old, she continued her active life. She travelled and often made inspection trips to the plantation at Grand Lake.[4]

Although usually quietly in the background of political affairs Mrs. Trapnall showed her patriotism in a dramatic act that has continued in the legends of the State. In 1861, Arkansas delegates met in a Secession Convention to consider the question of withdrawal from the Union. There were several who opposed secession, but when it became obvious that Arkansas' decision would be secession, the delegates moved to change their no votes and make Arkansas' decision unanimous. In the final vote only one man voted against secession. Isaac Murphy stood and spoke: "I have cast my vote after mature reflection, and have duly considered the consequences, and I cannot conscientiously change it. I therefore vote 'No."

At the conclusion of this speech, a bouquet of flowers landed at the feet of Isaac Murphy, tossed by Mrs. Frederic Trapnall from the gallery crowded with spectators.[5]

After this decisive gesture, Mrs. Trapnall resigned herself to the inevitable, and joined the other ladies of the city in preparing their men for war. Concerts, tableaux, and balls were given to raise money for aid to soldiers. Clothing was donated in Little Rock for Captain James B. Johnson's company in Kentucky.[6] Mrs. Trapnall's niece, Mary W. Cocke, was married to Captain Johnson. [7] The company was named the *Little Rock Grays* in honor of the ladies of Little Rock who had sent them many contributions. Before the company left Little Rock in June, Mrs. Trapnall had presented them with an embroidered battle flag, made by the Sisters of Mercy for the company. [8] The company enlisted for the duration of the war. Captain Johnson did not return from the war. He was killed near Murfreesboro, Tennessee on February 23, 1862.[9]

Mrs. Trapnall did not live to see the end of the war. Chicot County legend states that there is a lodestone in Lake Chicot that draws all those who have lived there back again.[10] At her country home in Chicot County Mrs. Trapnall became violently ill and died after a short sickness.[11] The *True Democrat* of January 9, 1862, took space away from news of the war to devote some gracious words to Mrs. Trapnall.

> The death of this estimable lady cast a gloom over the large circle of her friends and relations ... The death of one so kind-hearted, so talented and patriotic, is indeed a great loss and sad bereavement.[12]

Only one member of Frederic's immediate family, his daughter Mary Ringo Trapnall, now remained. She was put under the guardianship of Daniel Ringo. Judge Ringo's wife had died in 1859, also at Chicot County. He felt that it was more important that his wife's young namesake have a mother than a father. Therefore, he petitioned the court for permission to let Mary live with her closest female cousin, her mother's niece Mrs. James B. Johnson (Mary Watkins Cocke) at Trapnall Place. Apparently, Ringo was a fair administrator. The first two entries on the "Moneys Received for Account of the Estate of Frederic W. Trapnall" after the death of Mrs. Trapnall were an account of the "specie" she had in her possession at her death, and a $5.00 debt paid by Ringo for money he had borrowed from Martha at Grand Lake "just before her last illness."

The estate was now valued at from seventy to one hundred thousand dollars "if not greatly impaired in consequence of the existing Revolution."[13] The main portion consisted of lands and town lots. There were forty-two slaves, twenty-seven of whom were at Chicot County, and the remainder at Little Rock. Ringo sent the majority of the slaves to Chicot County

> ... where they will have constantly, proper treatment, provision and care and the children as they become able to work, be trained

and taught useful labor and preserved from contracting many vices to which they would be exposed if hired about from time to time for a series of years.[14]

Ringo also petitioned the court for permission to sell various lands and slaves of the estate at his discretion. In this petition, he describes "Trapnall Place, or Homestead of said Trapnall." He claims that extensive and somewhat expensive repairs were needed. "The roof is defective, ... and the outhouses, and fences, some of which have become very much dilapidated - so much so, that some of the fences are occasionally falling down;" Ringo suggests that the Homestead not be indiscrimately leased or rented to the highest bidder, but be let only to one who would be willing to do the necessary upkeep to preserve the home for Mary.[15] Subsequently Mrs. James B. Johnson and Mary moved into the house.

One piece of land Ringo sold was a 1120 acre farm in Pulaski County that Mrs. Trapnall had purchased. She had planned to move some of her workers from Chicot to this farm to cultivate it.[16] The plan was abandoned but it is testimony of her tremendous energy.

Much of the furniture of the estate was sold at public auction. Many of the best pieces were kept by Mrs. James B. Johnson for use in the house; others were reserved for Mary, including all of the silver, the mahogany bedroom furniture, most of the parlor furniture, bookcases and carpets.[17]

Mary, however, was not fated to carry on the name and traditions of her family. On August 22, 1863, she died at Curran Place.[18] Judge George Watkins was living at Curran Place at the time, married to Sophia Curran, widow of James Curran. They fled the house at the onset of the Civil War.[19]

Sold at Auction, on Account of H. Ring's
Administrator of the Estate of Mr. J. T. Trapnall

Jany 17	1 Set Knive Fork 14 & Steel		3 50
	2 Settees	16/	32 00
	1 Lounge		14 50
	1 Split Bottom Rocking Chair		7 25
	1 Rocking Chair		4 50
	1 Table		5 25
	1 Brass Kettle		4 50
	1 Large Iron Wash Kettle		15 50
	1 Refrigerator		35 00
	1 Pair Marble Tables Ea $21		42 00
	1 Clock		5 50
	2 Coal Oil Lamps	55	1 10
	1 Work Stand		12 50
	10 Arm Chairs	3.65	36 50
	1 Rocking Chair		13 50
	1 Large Marble Side Board		54 00
	1 Divan		45 00
	2 Pier Tables	$22.50	45 00
	1 Marble Top Centre Table		62 00
	1 " " " Wash Stand		35 00
	1 Plush Rocking Chair	$41.00	41 00
	1 Plush Rocking Chair		64 00
	1 What Not		7 50
	1 Cane Rocking Chair		15 00
	1 Piano		460 00
	50 lb Feathers	80 c	40 00
	38 " Feathers	70	26 60
	1 Mattrass		11 25
	1 Bed Stead & Cornice		26 00
	1 Spring Mattrass		12 50
	1 Bed Stead		6 00
		$1183.93	$1183 93

Estate auction: Trapnall probate file

Chapter XX

THE FATE OF TRAPNALL PLACE

Mary's heirs were her three surviving uncles: Benjamin Casey Trapnall, George Trapnall, and William V. Trapnall. All three of these brothers of Frederic were unmarried. Ben was appointed attorney-in-fact by the court, with his brothers' approval.[1]

On November 23, 1864, a destructive fire caused extensive damage on a block between the levee and Markham Street in downtown Little Rock. Many of the buildings destroyed were owned by those heirs of Frederic Trapnall's estate, who were still in Kentucky. The fire was later suspected to have been caused by an arsonist. Total losses of the property owners were reported at $50,000. The fire destroyed all but two buildings on the block.[2]

Ben delayed coming to Little Rock to probate the estate until after the Civil War, in 1865. It would not have been possible to settle the estate before even if he had been able to travel to Little Rock. He wrote to the Probate Court for permission to delay his arrival. Reasons he gave included the fact that Daniel Ringo, with whom he needed to talk, was out of town.[3] Ringo had left Little Rock before Federal troops took over the town, as had other confederate supporters. Ben was probably unwilling to travel in the war-ridden country and, possibly unable to pass through the battle lines to get to Little Rock.

He arrived late in 1865 and stayed in Little Rock for several years. Trapnall Place disappears from all records during these years. (It is neither on any list of dwellings used by Federal Troops, nor on a list of abandoned lands in the records of the Freeman's Bureau.) The conclusion is that Ben either used, rented or left it vacant. It reappears in records of 1869.

William Trapnall died in 1867, leaving only George and Ben as heirs.[4]

In June of 1869, George sold part of the square of Trapnall Block to Elizabeth P. Griffith.[5] In March of 1869, Ben sold another portion of Trapnall block to William E. and Ruth Woodruff. Neither of these sales included the homestead.[6]

On November 20, 1871, Trapnall Place passed from the hands of the Trapnall family. Ben and George deeded the land to Aylett B. Taylor.[7] At the time Ben was living in Little Rock at 309 East Fifth Street and practicing law.[8] Confusingly, the City Directory of 1871 also lists William Trapnall, an insurance agent, living at 309 East Fifth Street.[9] Since William V. Trapnall died in 1867,[10] this entry must refer to George Trapnall, living with his brother Ben in Little Rock.

Ben lived in Little Rock until 1872. Early that year, in failing health, he returned to Harrodsburg, Kentucky. On March 1, 1874, after a lingering illness, he died.[11]

Ben left good friends in Little Rock. The *Gazette* obituary for him said

> We are pained to learn through a private source of the death of Benjamin C. Trapnall, Esq.,... He was brother to the late Frederic W. Trapnall, one of Arkansas' most gifted and favorite sons, whom he much resembled in person and manner... Mr. Trapnall was a lawyer by profession, and an accomplished gentleman, and made many friends during his stay here, who will learn of his death with sincere regret.[12]

Ben left the money from a five thousand dollar life insurance policy to his church in Harrodsburg. He left a ten thousand dollar life insurance policy to his only surviving brother George. He also requested "to be buried in the New Cemetery at Harrodsburg, Mercer County, Kentucky, with a plain monument to mark the place with this inscription only on it: BENJAMIN CASEY TRAPNALL."[13] His request was honored, and he was buried at Spring Hill Cemetery.[14] Now all traces of his grave as well as of the graves of the rest of his family in Kentucky, are gone. A friend in Little Rock received an invitation to Ben's funeral, which was attended by all members of the Mercer County Bar.

Funeral Notice.

Yourself and family are invited to attend the funeral of

BENJAMIN C. TRAPNALL,

from the Morgan Hotel, to-morrow, afternoon, at 2 o'clock. Funeral services at the Episcopal church, by Rev. Mr. VENABLE. Interment at Spring Hill Cemetery.
HARRODSBURG, KY., March 2, 1874.

Aylett Taylor was seventy years old at the time when he and his wife Rebecca White Taylor bought Trapnall Place.[15] They had a son and two daughters. The son died in 1866.[16] Both daughters, Sallie and Rebecca Aylett, married. Sallie had died in 1860. Her husband, Ben T. Embry, and their two children, Aylett and Rebecca Katherine, did however, live at Trapnall Place. Ben T. Embry served as acting governor from September 25 through 30, 1883, during the term of Governor James H. Berry. Rebecca Katherine Embry married Dr. Andrew Homer Scott, grandson of territorial Judge Andrew Scot, in Trapnall Hall on May 2, 1877.

Rebecca Aylett Taylor, married Robert Allen Dowdle, a grocer and liquor dealer. The Dowdle family lived in Trapnall Place except during the 1870s. There were nine Dowdle children, some of whom were born and all of whom lived at Trapnall Place.

Aylett Taylor and his wife lived in Trapnall Place until their deaths. However, six years before his death, Aylett deeded half-interest in the house to his daughter Rebecca Aylett Taylor and half-interest to the two children of Sallie, Aylett Embry and Rebecca Katherine Embry.

Eventually Rebecca Aylett Taylor and her husband Robert Allen Dowdle purchased all of the interest in the house. They came into full possession of it on December 28, 1885. On September 30, 1894, they sold Trapnall Place to Charles A. Carroll and his children. The Carrolls were said to be relatives of the Trapnall family. One of their children was named Fannie Trapnall Carroll, one Nicholas Casey Carroll. Their other children were Susie Carroll and Irene Carroll. All of this family lived in the old Trapnall home. Charles and his son Nicholas Casey worked for Union Compress Company; Irene and Susie were students. Fannie, Irene and Susie moved to Baltimore, Maryland in the late 1890s. Charles and his son stayed at Trapnall Place until 1899, when they moved to New Orleans.

Trapnall Place was rented between 1899 and 1903 and it began to fall into disrepair. Then, in November of 1904, C. R. Shinault and his wife Josephine Pillow Shinault, bought Trapnall Place. The Shinaults had moved from Helena, Arkansas. Shinault was a physician; his partner was Doctor J. P. Runyan.[17] Their daughter, Josephine Pillow Shinault Thompson, was born at Trapnall Place in 1908. She lives today in Helena in her mother's family home - the Pillow House.

Dr. Shinault built an office on the east side of the house, which by this time had many additions. There was also now a two story brick carriage house on the west side of the house, with a circular drive leading to it. The top story of the carriage house was connected to the main house. It is not thought that the carriage house was original.

Dr. Shinault was interested in exotic animals. He kept a menagerie fenced in behind the house. Among his animals were lambs, deer, peacocks and pigeons.

In 1916 a destructive fire occurred at Trapnall Place. The Shinaults stayed at the Rainwater Apartments while repairs were made. Mr. and Mrs. Sunny Dickinson, a recently married couple, were renting part of the east wing at the time of the fire.

During repairs some changes were made in the structure. The most significant was lowering the ceilings by three feet. The beautiful brass gas chandeliers which had hung in the parlors were twisted and blackened by the fire. No attempt was made to restore them; they were simply tossed into the attic - not to be discovered until 1963.

The Shinaults returned to Helena not long after this, but retained ownership of the house. It was again rented out and used as a boarding house. At one time it reportedly had as many as seventeen rooms and five baths. During this period Andrew V. Smith, United States ambassador to the Phillipines, and Rutledge Hawn and his brothers, father and uncles to actress and comedianne Goldie Hawn, lived at Trapnall Place.

From approximately 1926 to 1929, it was a fraternity house for the Medical School fraternity of Chi Zeta Chi. According to members of the fraternity, the house was in a run-down condition when the fraternity moved into it. At that time it was a two-story structure, the second story apparently added after the 1916 fire. It is not clear whether the house had been painted red at this time or was still natural brick. Fraternity members memories differ on this point and pictures of the house from this time are not clear enough to settle the question.

The fraternity held dances in the large central hallway, which had always been the center of entertainment in the house. They had a house-mother and a house-maid to watch over the young men and cook and clean for them. The fraternity was the last occupant of the house before the Junior League gained possession of it.

C. R. Shinault died before his wife. He left most of his property to her. In his will he suggested that she tear down his residence at 423 East Capitol and build an apartment building to provide income for herself and their daughter. This was not done.

Members of Chi Zeta Chi in front of Trapnall Place

Chapter XXI

TRAPNALL HALL

Mrs. Shinault sold the property to V. C. Johnson in December of 1928.[1] Johnson also had plans to tear down the house. This came to the attention of Julia Taylor, who bought the property on January 28, 1929, to prevent its destruction.[2] She immediately deeded Trapnall Place to the Junior League of Little Rock as a memorial to her husband, Dr. Charles Minor Taylor. She specified that the house always be used for welfare work.[3]

The March 24, 1929 edition of the *Arkansas Democrat* was sponsored by the Junior League. All profits from the edition were to go to the League to help in "equipping its new home."[4] Junior League members were featured in most of the ads in the paper, modelling clothes under headlines such as "The Junior Leaguer Comes to Cohn's For Her Clothes," and demonstrating appliances, "Junior League Members approve Frigidaire For Health, Convenience, Economy, Silent Operation." Mrs. Whitney Harb was the Junior League president at this time.[5]

Miss Elizabeth Taylor was chairman of the Junior League's committee on the Taylor Memorial.[6] Eight members were put in charge of reconstructing their new home: Miss Rose Lafferty, Mrs. C. K. Lincoln, Mrs. Deadrick Cantrell, Mrs. R. M. Williams, Miss Louise Alexandre, Miss Betty Galloway, Miss Elizabeth Taylor and Miss Katherine Lyon.[7] The architectural firm of Thompson, Sanders and Ginocchio donated its services. They "evolved plans which preserve the original colonial lines of the exterior while the inside is designed to meet modern welfare requirements."[8] The architects did not, in fact, attempt any restoration of the exterior.

The west of the home was used for child welfare work, the east for meeting rooms and offices. The large hall, as always, was used for bigger gatherings. There was still a large sunporch on the southern end of the house which was enclosed to be used as a playroom and sun room for the children served at the welfare offices.[9]

The official name of the headquarters of the Junior League at this time was the Doctor Charles M. Taylor Memorial.

Trapnall Place served as the headquarters of the Junior League for over thirty years. At this time, the League members decided that something major should be done about the house.

In 1962, Mrs. Austin McCaskill was President of the Little Rock Junior League.[10] The League considered the alternatives concerning Trapnall Hall. They could sell it or tear it down. Several of the members, among them Peg Smith, suggested restoration. She consulted architectural historian John V. Robinson who encouraged the idea.[11] The plan fit in neatly with the Little Rock Housing Authority's newly-aroused concern to restore and preserve Little Rock's downtown nineteenth century historical and architectural heritage. The Little Rock Housing Authority's seven-member technical advisory committee encouraged and gave technical help to the Junior League when they made the commitment to restore their headquarters as closely as possible to its original state. It became the pilot project in the Quapaw Quarter program of restoration and preservation.[12] The house was officially closed in April of 1963, and the work of restoration was begun with John Truemper architect, Fred Parrot builder, Eloise Murphy decorator, and Robert Rohde landscape architect.[13]

The gas chandeliers that had been stored in the attic after the 1916 fire were discovered at this time. The brass chandeliers were manufactured by the company of Cornelius and Baker in Philadelphia circa 1850.[14] The lights possibly are original to the house and were used by the Trapnalls. Although Little Rock did not have piped gas until around 1860, individual homes among the wealthier citizens had their personal coal gas generators, and such was apparently the case with the Trapnall family.

Every effort was made at this time to return Trapnall Place to its original condition. All additions were torn down, leaving again the basic symmetrical design of the home. The only addition not original is a catering kitchen and storerooms across the back of the house where the sunporch originally was. The partition between the two east parlors was removed to make a large meeting room. Doors that had originally led out to the southern porch were either closed off, or used as doors into the hallway and the kitchen. The two windows on the south wall of the original dining room and bedrooms were closed up.

The house was formally reopened seven months later on Friday, November 1, 1963. An opening ceremony was held with Miss Julia Taylor, granddaughter of Mrs. Charles M. Taylor, as ribbon cutter.[15]

Trapnall Hall, renamed such by the Junior League, served as its headquarters until 1976. In this year the Arkansas Commemorative Commission acquired Trapnall Hall. The Junior League donated half of the appraised value of Trapnall Hall while a grant from the National Park Service administered through the Arkansas Historic Preservation Program made up the other half. Trapnall Hall was then designated as the Governor's Official Receiving Hall. It is now available to Arkansans for private functions.

During restoration, 1963

Trapnall Hall, 1980

Inscription on tombstone:

The silver cord is loosened, the golden bow is broken,
The pitcher is broken at the fountain
The wheel is broken at the cistern
Dust returns to dust, and the spirit to God who gave it.

A found and true husband, A devoted father,
A dutiful and loving son, an affectionate brother, a faithful friend
Sleeps here.

In the prime of manhood and the full vigour of an ample and cultivated
intellect,
He was taken away.

Devoted to the welfare of his country,
He died in her service,
A victum to his untiring zeal.

Eminent as a lawyer, he was an ornament to his profession,
Possessing the esteem, respect, and admiration of his associates.[18]

EPILOGUE

So we bring the story to the present. The Bar Association of Arkansas and the House of Representatives follow procedures that Frederic Trapnall helped to establish. The actions of Martha Francis Trapnall, reflecting her strong political beliefs and her able management of the family estate after the death of her husband were significant in an era when women were not expected to have or show such views. Although there are many things we do not know about the Trapnalls, much of what we do know comes to us through their home. After many years and many owners, Trapnall Place, now known as Trapnall Hall, stands basically as it did in the days of the Trapnalls. As the Governor's Official Receiving Hall, it is again a setting for entertaining those prominent in the government of our state. The faces and the dress are different now; the atmosphere, the elegance, are as they were. The Trapnall family's rich heritage continues today in Trapnall Hall.

NOTES

CHAPTER I

[1]Tombstone Inscription of Frederic W. Trapnall, Mount Holly Cemetery, Little Rock, Arkansas.

[2]Letter received from Brian Austin, Trapnell Family Historian, August 13, 1979, TSL.

[3]G. H. Spillman, M.D., "Biographical Sketch of Philip Trapnall, M.D." read before the State Medical Association of Kentucky, Bardstown, Kentucky, April 18, 1860. (Collected Papers of Brian Austin)

[4]Letter received from Brian Austin, Trapnell Family Historian, August 13, 1979, TLS.

[5]Brian Austin, Trapnell Family Historian, letter to Carolyn Grimes, Harrodsburg Historical Society, September 27, 1977, ALS.

CHAPTER II

[1]Spillman.

[2]*Ibid.*

[3]Marriage Records, Mercer County, Kentucky, Mercer County Courthouse, Harrodsburg, Kentucky, Book 1, p. 116.

[4]Spillman.

[5]*Journal of the Kentucky House of Representatives,* Seventh Session (1834 - 1835).

[6]*Ibid.*

[7]Spillman.

[8]*Ibid.*

[9]*Ibid.*

[10]*Ibid.*

[11]*Ibid.*

[12]*Ibid.*

[13]*Ibid.*

[14]Letter from Isaac Pearson of Harrodsburg, Kentucky, to Dr. R. W. Trapnall, Point of Rocks, Maryland, 1898. (Collected Papers of Brian Austin)

[15]Spillman.

[16]*Ibid.*

[17]*Ibid.*

[18]1820 Census, Mercer County, Kentucky, Arkansas History Commission, Little Rock, Arkansas.

[19]Will Book, Mercer County, 1847, Mercer County Courthouse, Harrodsburg, Kentucky, Book 14, pp. 139-140.

[20]*Ibid.*

[21]Maria T. Daviess, *History of Mercer and Boyle Counties, Vol. I.* (Harrodsburg, Kentucky: The Harrodsburg Herald, 1924), p. 85.

[22]*Ibid.* p. 90.

[23]Will Book, Mercer County, Mercer County Courthouse, Harrodsburg, Kentucky, Book 14, p. 321.

[24]Annotated family trees. (Collected Papers of Brian Austin)

[25]*Arkansas Banner,* January 16, 1844, p.2., col. 3.

[26]*Ibid.*

[27]*Ibid.*

[28]Annotated family trees. (Collected Papers of Brian Austin)

[29]*Ibid.*

[30]*Arkansas Gazette,* July 10, 1839, p.2., col. 3.

[31]*Ibid.*

[32]1850 Census, Union County, Kentucky, Arkansas History Commission, Little Rock, Arkansas.

[33]Abstract of Title for Trapnall Hall, Beach Abstract and Guaranty Company, Little Rock, Arkansas.

[34]*Arkansas Gazette*, March 10, 1874, p.1., col. 1.

[35]Daviess, p. 85.

[36]*Arkansas Gazette*, March 17, 1874, p.4., col. 4.

[37]Daviess, p. 159.

[38]*Ibid.* p. 84

[39]*Ibid.*

[40]Samuel Eliot Morison, *Oxford History of the American People,* (New York: Oxford University Press, 1965).

[41]Pamphlet on "St. Philip's Episcopal Church, Short and Chiles Streets, Harrodsburg, Kentucky 40330," (Restoration committee).

[42]*Ibid.*

[43]*Ibid.*

[44]Tombstone Inscription of Frederic W. Trapnall, Mount Holly Cemetery, Little Rock, Arkansas.

[45]Daviess, p. 143.

[46]Ramol Henry, Archivist, Transylvania College, Letter to Barbara Brigance, February 16, 1978.

[47]Daviess, p. 147.

[48]*Ibid.* p. 90.

[49]*Ibid.* p. 143.

CHAPTER III

[1]Tax Book, Washington County Courthouse, Springfield, Kentucky, 1829.

[2]Marriage Bonds, Washington County Courthouse, Springfield, Kentucky.

[3]*Kentucky Supreme Court Reports,* Vol. 33, Fall term 1835, Isaacs vs. Taylor, p. 600.

[4]*Journal of the Kentucky House of Representatives* (1834 - 1835)

[5]Records of Nazareth Academy, Nazareth, Kentucky, received in letter from Carolyn H. Grimes, President of Harrodsburg Historical Society, November 30, 1979. Nazareth College closed about 1965, and is now used as housing for retired faculty.

[6]Virginia Webb Cocke, *Cockes and Cousins, Vol. II: Descendants of Thomas Cocke c. 1639 - 1897* (Ann Arbor, Michigan: Edwards Brothers, Inc., 1974), p. 30.

CHAPTER IV

[1]*Ibid.* p. 30. All the following information about the Cocke family comes from this source unless otherwise cited.

[2]*Ibid.,* p. 30.

[3]1850 Census, Pulaski County, Arkansas, Arkansas History Commission, Little Rock, Arkansas.

[4]Tombstone Inscription of Richard Philip Trapnall, Mount Holly Cemetery, Little Rock, Arkansas.

[5]Cocke, p. 30.

[6]Records of Nazareth Academy, Nazareth, Kentucky.

[7]Ira Don Richards, *Story of A Rivertown* (United States: Privately printed, 1969), p. 120.

[8]*Arkansas Advocate*, May 8, 1835.

[9]Richards, p. 11.

[10]Albert Pike, "Letters from Arkansas," American Monthly Magazine (Jan., 1836), p. 30.

[11]*Ibid.*

[12]*Arkansas Advocate*, March 19, 1822.

[13]Boyd W. Johnson, *The Arkansas Frontier* (United States: privately printed, 1957), p. 105.

[14]*Ibid.*

[15]*Ibid.*

[16]Richards, p. 18.

[17]*Arkansas Gazette*, March 3, 1835.

[18]*Arkansas Gazette*, November 24, 1830.

[19]*Arkansas Gazette*, November 1, 1850, p.4., col. 4.

[20]1840 Census, Pulaski County, Arkansas, Arkansas History Commission, Little Rock, Arkansas.

[21]Tombstone Inscription of Richard Philip Trapnall, Mount Holly Cemetery, Little Rock, Arkansas.

CHAPTER V

[1]*Arkansas Gazette*, November 29, 1850, p.2., col. 6.

[2]*Constitution of the Bar Association of the State of Arkansas, Adopted at an Aggregate Meeting of the Profession Held in the City of Little Rock on the 24th day of November, 1837* (Little Rock: Woodruff and Pew, 1838), p.12.

[3]*Ibid.*

[4]John Hallum, *Biographical and Pictoral History of Arkansas, Vol. I.,* (Albany: Weed, Parsons and Co. Printers, 1887), p. 93.

[5]Judge William F. Pope, *Early Days in Arkansas* (Little Rock: Frederick W. Allsopp, 1895), p. 217.

[6]Constitution of the Bar Association, p.3.

[7]*Ibid.*, p.6.

[8]*Ibid.*, p.7.

[9]*Ibid.*, p.7-8.

[10]*Ibid.*, p.10.

[11]Pope, p. 215.

[12]*Arkansas Supreme Court Report,* Vol. I (January 1838) through Vol. VII (January and July terms 1846, and January term 1847).

[14]George B. Rose, "Previous Bar Associations in Arkansas," *Proceedings of the 35th Annual Meeting of the Bar Association of Arkansas held at Hot Spring, Arkansas, May 26 and 27, 1932.*

[13]Cocke, p. 30.

[15]*Arkansas Gazette*, December 11, 1839, p.2., col.4.

[16]Richards, p.30.

[17]*Ibid.* p. 31.

CHAPTER VI

[1]Ellen H. Cantrell, *Annals of Christ Church Parish from A.D. 1839 to A.D. 1899* (Little Rock: Arkansas Democrat Company, 1900), p. 43.

[2]*Ibid.* p. 11.

[3]Fay Hempstead, *Reminiscences of Christ Church: An Address Delivered by Mr. Fay Hempstead, July 20, 1924,* p. 11.

[4]*Ibid.* p. 11.

[5]Cantrell, p. 74.

[6]Margaret Simms McDonald, *White Already to Harvest: The Episcopal Church in Arkansas, 1838-1971* (Sewanee, Tennessee: University Press, 1975), p. 25.

[7]McDonald, p. 25.

[8]McDonald, p. 451   Also Cantrell, p. 11.

[9]*Ibid.*

[10]*Ibid.*

[11]McDonald, p. 22.

[12]*Ibid.*

[13]*Ibid.* p. 27.

[14]Hempstead, p. 12.

[15]Cantrell, p. 85.

[16]Records of Nazareth Academy, Nazareth, Kentucky.

[17]McDonald, p. 27.

[18]Hempstead, p. 15.

CHAPTER VII

[1]Abstract of Title of Trapnall Hall, Beach Abstract and Guaranty Company, Little Rock, Arkansas.

[2]"The ground on which Trapnall Hall stands was part of 3500 acres given by the Quapaw Indians to a French family by the name of Imbeau in 1797; this generous gesture was made because the Imbeaus had aided the Quapaws in their tribal war against the Osage Indians. On June 20, 1820, this verbal transfer was ratified by a long wordy document at a pompous powwow of the Quapaws, was signed by their chief and witnessed by two residents of Little Rock, Moses Austin and Dr. Matthew Cunningham. This deed stated that one of the younger Imbeau men had recently married a sister of the Quapaw Chief, Heckaton, so the gift was probably a dower or bridal gift." This same information appears many times in the various papers I have collected about Trapnall Place. It is not documented in any of those places, and seems to have originated with an aritcle written by Elizabeth Taylor in the March 24, 1929, *Arkansas Democrat*, and in a speech that she gave to the Junior League. In the absense of further documentation this information cannot be substantiated at present. With the help of Ann Edmiston I have verified that some of the Imbeau family, a half-French, half-Quapaw family, did at one time have land in the general area of Trapnall Place.

[3]Abstract of Title.

[4]*Ibid.*

[5]Probate File, Frederic W. Trapnall, Arkansas History Commission, Little Rock, Arkansas.

[6]*Ibid.*

[7]Tax records, Pulaski County, 1942, Arkansas History Commission, Little Rock, Arkansas.

[8]"The Crittenden Home," *Arkansas Advocate,* May 30, 1832.

[9]Wilson Stiles, personal interview, April 19, 1980.

[10]Wilson Stiles, "Kentucky Architect First to Design Arkansas Building," The Quapaw Quarter Chronicle, *April, 1978, p. 8.*

[11]*Arkansas Gazette* October 23, 1844, p.3., col. 4.

[12]Probate File, Frederic W. Trapnall, Arkansas History Commission, Little Rock, Arkansas.

[13]*Ibid.*

[14]Probate File, Frederic W. Trapnall, "Inventory and Appraisement of Slaves and Other Personal Property Belonging to Estate of Frederic W. Trapnall," Arkansas History Commission, Little Rock, Arkansas. All following information about personal belongings of the Trapnall family are from this source unles otherwise cited.

[15]Trapnall Hall Nomination for National Register, prepared by John V. Robinson, October 20, 1972. Also Memorandum from Cromwell, Neyland, Truemper, Levy and Gatchell to Barbara Brigance, June 10, 1977.

[16]Tombstone Inscription of Mary Ringo Trapnall, Mount Holly Cemetery, Little Rock, Arkansas.

[17]Memorandum from Cromwell, Neyland, Truemper, Levy and Gatchell to Barbara Brigance, June 10, 1977.

[18]Manuscript Map "Bird's Eye View of the City of Little Rock, The Capitol of Arkansas," 1871.

[19]Trapnall Hall Nomination for National Register, prepared by John V. Robinson, October 20, 1972. Also Memorandum from Cromwell, Neyland, Truemper, Levy and Gatchell to Barbara Brigance, June 10, 1977.

[20]*True Democrat.* November 21, 1857.

[21]Probate file of Frederic Trapnall.

[22]Pope, p. 254.

[23]Probate file of Frederic Trapnall.

[24]Arkansas Census, Pulaski County, 1850, Arkansas History Commission, Little Rock, Arkansas.

CHAPTER VIII

[1]*Arkansas Supreme Court Reports,* Vol. 7, 1846 - 1847.

[2]*Arkansas Supreme Court Reports,* Vol. 6, 1845 - 1846.

[3]*Arkansas Supreme Court Reports,* Vol. 8, 1847 - 1848.

[4]Hallum, p. 89.

[5]*Ibid.*

[6]*Ibid.* p. 75.

CHAPTER IX

[1]Deed Book, Chicot County, Chicot County Courthouse, Lake Village, Arkansas, Document number D-418.

[2]*Ibid.* Document number E-230.

[3]*Ibid.* Document number E-39.

[4]*Ibid.* Document number E-397.

[5]*Ibid.* Document number E-340.

[6]*Ibid.* Document number F-451.

[7]Mrs. W. Garland Street, "Chicot County Historical Sketch," Place File, Arkansas History Commission, Little Rock, Arkansas. According to Mrs. Street, this is information furnished her in a loose leaf history of Arkansas, whose author is unknown and which is now out of print.

[8]*Ibid.*

[9]Deed Book, Chicot County, Chicot County Courthouse, Lake Village, Arkansas, Document number F-451.

[10]Probate file of Frederic Trapnall.

[11]Tax Books, Jefferson County, Jefferson County Courthouse, Pine Bluff, Arkansas, 1851 and 1852.

[12]Tax Books, Pulaski County, Pulaski County Courthouse, Little Rock, Arkansas, 1840 - 1848.

[13]Probate File of Frederic Trapnall.

CHAPTER X

[1]*Arkansas Gazette,* November 15, 1843, p.2., col. 3.

[2]*Ibid.*

[3]*Arkansas Gazette,* December 27, 1843, p.3., col. 1.

[4]*Arkansas Gazette,* December 27, 1843, p.2., col. 1.

[5]*Arkansas Gazette,* January 3, 1844, p.2., col. 3.

[6]*Ibid.*

[7]*Arkansas Gazette,* January 19, 1844, p.2., col. 2.

[8]*Arkansas Gazette,* January 19, 1844, p.2., col. 2.

[9]*Arkansas Banner,* January 23, 1844.

[10]Pope, pp. 256-257.

[11]Margaret Smith Ross, *Arkansas Gazette: The Early Years 1819 - 1866* (Little Rock: Arkansas Gazette Foundation, 1969), p. 186.

[12]*Arkansas Gazette,* August 28, 1844, p.2., col. 5.

[13]*Ibid.*

[14]*Arkansas Gazette,* August 28, 1844, p.2., col. 3.

[15]*Arkansas Gazette,* August 28, 1844, p.2., col. 2.

[16]*Arkansas Gazette,* March 27, 1844, p.3., col. 5.

CHAPTER XI

[1]Journal of the Arkansas House of Representatives, Fifth Session. All information in the following section is taken from this source unless otherwise cited.

[2]*Ibid.,* p. 247.

[3]*Ibid.*

[4]*Arkansas Gazette,* June 8, 1846, p.2., col. 3.

CHAPTER XII

[1]Pope, p. 115.

[2]Pope, p. 115.

[3]Ross, *Arkansas Gazette: The Early Years,* p. 202.

[4]*Ibid.*

[5]*Ibid.*

[6]*Ibid.*

CHAPTER XIII

[1]*Journal of the Arkansas House of Representatives,* Seventh Session (November 6, 1848 - January 10, 1849), All information in the following section comes from this source unless otherwise cited.

[2]*Arkansas Democrat,* December 8, 1848.

[3]Journal of the House of Representatives, Seven Session p. 170, p. 221.

CHAPTER XIV

[1]Ramol Henry, Archivist, Transylvania College, letter to Barbara Brigance, February 16, 1978.

[2]*Arkansas Gazette,* July 27, 1848.

[3]*Arkansas Supreme Court Reports,* Vol. 9, 1848 - 1849.

[4]*Arkansas Supreme Court Reports,* Vol. 12, 1841 - 1842.

CHAPTER XV

[1]*Journal of the Arkansas House of Representatives,* Eighth Session (November 4, 1850 - January 13, 1851). All following information in this section comes from this source unless otherwise cited.

CHAPTER XVI

[1]Marriage Books, Pulaski County, Arkansas History Commission, Little Rock, Arkansas, Book 1, p. 67.

[2]Margaret Smith Ross, "Sanford C. Faulkner," *The Arkansas Historical Quarterly,* 14 No. 4 (1955), p. 301.

[3]Civil Appointments, City of Little Rock, Pulaski County, Arkansas History Commission, Little Rock, Arkansas.

[4]Tax Books, Pulaski County, Arkansas History Commission, Little Rock, Arkansas.

[5]Probate File, Philip Trapnall, "Inventory of Estate," June 9, 1857, Arkansas History Commission, Little Rock, Arkansas. All the following information comes from this source unless otherwise cited.

[6]*True Democrat,* December 9, 1856.

[7]Will Book, Pulaski County, Arkansas History Commission, Little Rock, Arkansas, Book B, pp. 118-119. Also Probate File, Philip Trapnall.

[8]Tax Books, Pulaski County, Arkansas History Commission, Little Rock, Arkansas, 1857.

[9]"No Longer a Belle: The Sad Story of 'The Most Beautiful Woman in Arkansas.' " *Arkansas Gazette,* March 5, 1880, p. 2., col. 1.

[10]Marriage Records, Pulaski County, Arkansas History Commission, Little Rock, Arkansas, Book 1, p. 67.

[11]Ross, "Sanford C. Faulkner."

[12]"No Longer a Belle."

[13]Tombstone of Mary Ringo Trapnall, Mount Holly Cemetery, Little Rock, Arkansas.

[14]*Spirit of the Times,* New York, New York, February 21, 1852, p. 7.

[15]*Arkansas Gazette,* June 3, 1852, p.1., col. 5.

CHAPTER XVII

[1]*Arkansas Whig*, May 19, 1853, p. 2., col. 5.
[2]*Arkansas Whig*, May 19, 1853, p. 2., col. 6.
[3]*Ibid.*
[4]*Ibid.*
[5]*Ibid.*
[6]*Ibid.*
[7]*Ibid.*
[8]*Ibid.*
[9]*Arkansas Whig*, July 7, 1853.
[10]*Arkansas Gazette*, March 3, 1835.
[11]*Arkansas Gazette*, July 23, 1852, p.3., col. 6 - 7.
[12]*Arkansas Gazette*, July 23, 1852, p.3., col. 6.
[13]*Arkansas Gazette*, May 20, 1853, p.2., col. 1.
[14]*Arkansas Gazette*, June 24, 1853, p.2., col. 1.
[15]*Arkansas Gazette*, June 2, 1853.
[16]*Arkansas True Democrat*, June 21, 1853, p.2., col. 3.
[17]*Arkansas Gazette*, June 10, 1853.
[18]*Arkansas Whig*, June 16, 1853.
[19]*Arkansas Gazette*, June 17, 1853.
[20]*Journal of the House*, Seventh Session, p. 301.
[21]*Acts of Arkansas* (1844 to 1850), p. 173.
[22]*Arkansas Whig*. June 16, 1853, p.2., col. 1.

CHAPTER XVIII

[1]*Arkansas Gazette*, July 1, 1853, p.2., col. 3.
[2]Probate File of Frederic W. Trapnall.
[3]*Arkansas Whig*, July 7, 1853.
[4]*Arkansas Gazette*, July 8, 1853, p.2., col. 3.
[5]*Arkansas Gazette*, July 15, 1853, p.3., col. 1-2.
[6]Tombstone of Frederic Trapnall, Mount Holly Cemetery, Little Rock, Arkansas.
[7]*Arkansas Whig*, July 7, 1853.
[8]*Arkansas Gazette*, July 8, 1853.
[9]Probate File of Frederic Trapnall.
[10]*True Democrat*, July 5, 1853, p.2., col. 1.
[11]*Arkansas Gazette*, July 8, 1853, p.2., col. 3.

[12]*Arkansas Gazette*, July 8, 1853.

[13]*Arkansas Gazette*, July 8, 1853, p.2., col. 3.

[14]*Arkansas Gazette*, July 15, 1853, p.3., col. 1-2.

[15]*Ibid.*

[16]George B. Rose, "The Bar of Early Arkansas," *Proceedings of the Bar Association of Arkansas (Sixth Annual Meeting),* Little Rock, Arkansas, May 26 - 27, 1903, p. 38.

[17]*Arkansas Gazette*, July 15, 1853.

[18]Tombstone Inscription of Frederic Trapnall.

CHAPTER XIX

[1]Will Book, Frederic Trapnall, Pulaski County, Arkansas History Commission, Little Rock, Arkansas.

[2]*Ibid.*

[3]*Ibid.*

[4]Probate File, Frederic Trapnall.

[5]*Arkansas Gazette*, May 11, 1861.

[6]Margaret Smith Ross, "Negroes Do Their Part In Fund-Raising Drives," Chronicles of Arkansas, *Arkansas Gazette*, November 14, 1961, p. 6B.

[7]Marriage Records, Pulaski County, Arkansas

[8]Ross, "Negroes Do Their Part In Fund-Raising Drives."

[9]*Arkansas Gazette*, February 23, 1862.

[10]Street.

[11]Tombstone Inscription of Mrs. Martha Trapnall, Mount Holly Cemetery, Little Rock, Arkansas.

[12]*True Democrat*, January 9, 1862, p.2., col.1.

[13]Probate file of Frederic Trapnall.

[14]*Ibid.*

[15]*Ibid.*

[16]*Ibid.*

[17]*Ibid.*

[18]Tombstone Inscription of Mary Trapnall, Mount Holly Cemetery, Little Rock, Arkansas.

[19]Curran Hall Nomination for National Register, prepared by Mike Shinn, September 9, 1975.

CHAPTER XX

[1]Probate File of Martha Trapnall, Arkansas History Commission, Little Rock, Arkansas.

[2]Margaret Smith Ross, "Chronicles of Arkansas," *Arkansas Gazette*, November 23, 1964, p.6., cols. 1-2

[3]Probate File of Martha Trapnall.

[4]Will Books, Will of Dr. Philip Trapnall, Mercer County Courthouse, Harrodsburg, Kentucky, Book 14, p. 139.

[5]Abstract of Title.

[6]*Ibid.*

[7]*Ibid.*

[8]City Directory of the City of Little Rock, 1871, Arkansas History Commission, Little Rock, Arkansas.

[9]*Ibid.*

[10]Will of Dr. Philip.

[11]*Arkansas Gazette,* March 10, 1874, p.1., col. 1.

[12]*Ibid.*

[13]Will Books, Will of Benjamin Casey Trapnall, Mercer County Courthouse, Harrodsburg, Kentucky, Book 18, p. 173.

[14]Engraved invitation to funeral of Benjamin Trapnall, sent to Little Rock, 1874.

[15]Abstract of Title.

[16]All following information from Abstract of Title of Trapnal Hall, also Ross, "Trapnall Hall," *Pulaski County Historical Review,* December, 1955.

[17]Mrs. Francis Thompson, Telephone interview, July 16, 1979.

CHAPTER XXI

[1]*Ibid.*

[2]*Ibid.*

[3]*Ibid.*

[4]*Arkansas Democrat,* March 24, 1929, p.1., col. 5.

[5]*Ibid.*

[6]*Ibid.*

[7]*Ibid.*

[8]*Ibid.*

[9]*Ibid.*

[10]*Ibid.*

[11]John V. Robinson, personal interview, January 28, 1977.

[12]John Robinson, "Little Rock's Quapaw Quarter," *Profile*, Fall, 1968.

[13]"History of the Dr. Charles Minor Taylor Memorial," *The Junior League of Little Rock, Inc., Area V. Yearbook, 1974 - 1975*, p. 15.

[14]Roger Moss, personal interview, November 17, 1979.

[15]"History of the Dr. Charles Minor Taylor Memorial," p. 15.

BIBLIOGRAPHY

I. PRIMARY SOURCES

Newspapers

Arkansas Advocate, Little Rock, Arkansas, 1832.

Arkansas Banner, Little Rock, Arkansas, 1844.

Arkansas Democrat, Little Rock, Arkansas, 1848, 1879, 1929

Arkansas Gazette, (title varies), Little Rock, Arkansas, 1824 - 1874, 1944,
      1956 - 1979.

Arkansas True Democrat, Little Rock, Arkansas, 1856, 1862.

Arkansas Whig, Little Rock, Arkansas, 1853.

Spirit of the Times, New York, New York, 1852.

Public Records

Arkansas Civil Appointments, Records of the State, Arkansas History
      Commission, Little Rock, Arkansas.

Arkansas Freedmen's Bureau. List of Abandoned and Confiscated
      Lands 1865 - 1868. Arkansas History Commission,
      Little Rock, Arkansas.

Arkansas General Assembly. *Acts, Memorials and Resolutions passed
      at the Fifth Session of the General Assembly of the
State of Arkansas.* Little Rock: 1844.

——————. *Acts, Memorials and Resolutions passed at the Eighth
      Session of the General Assembly of the State of Arkansas.*
      Little Rock: 1851.

——————. *Arkansas Journal of the House of Representatives,*
      Fifth Session: 4 November 1844 - 10 January 1845.

——————. *Arkansas Journal of the House of Representatives,*
      Seventh Session: 6 November 1848 - 10 January 1849.

——————. *Arkansas Journal of the House of Representatives,*
      Eighth Session: 4 November 1850 - 13 January 1851.

Arkansas Supreme Court. *Reports of Cases,* Vols. 1 - 13, 15.

Chicot County, Arkansas. Deed Books. Lake Village, Arkansas.

Constitution of the Bar Association of the State of Arkansas, Adopted
      at an Aggregate Meeting of the Profession,
      Held in the City of Little Rock, on the 24th of
      November, 1837. Little Rock: Woodruff and Pew, 1838.

Jefferson County, Arkansas. Tax Records, 1851, 1852.

Kentucky General Assembly. *Journal of the House of Representatives,*
  1805 - 06

——————. *Journal of the House of Representatives,*
1806 - 07.

——————. *Journal of the House of Representatives,*
1834 - 35.

Kentucky Supreme Court. *Reports of Cases,* Vol. 33.

Little Rock City Directories: 1871, 1872, 1873, 1876, 1877, 1880,
  1881, 1910, 1913, 1924, 1928, 1929.

Mercer County, Kentucky. Marriage Bonds and Consents.

——————. Will Books: 4, 5, 9, 14, 15, 16, 18, 24, 25,
  29, 30, 46.

Nazareth Academy, Nazareth, Kentucky. Selected Student Records of
  Nazareth Academy.

Pulaski County, Arkansas. Probate Court Files of Frederic W. Trapnall,
  Martha Frances Trapnall, Benjamin Casey Trapnall,
  and George Trapnall.

——————. Tax Records: 1839, 1840, 1841, 1842, 1847, 1848, 1851,
  1867, 1868, 1869.

——————. Will Book B.

Report of the Proceedings of the Bar Association of Arkansas at the
  Sixth Annual Meeting held at Little Rock, Arkansas.
  May 26 and 27, 1903.

Report of the Proceedings of the Bar Association of Arkansas at the
  Thirty-fifth Annual Meeting held at Hot Springs,
Arkansas. May 26 and 27, 1932.

Transylvania College, Lexington, Kentucky. Selected Student Records
  of Transylvania College.

United States Census, Chicot County, Arkansas: 1860.

United States Census, Mercer County, Kentucky: 1790, 1800, 1810,
  1820, 1830, 1840, 1850.

United States Census, Pulaski County, Arkansas: 1840, 1850,
  1860, 1870.

United States Census, Union County, Kentucky: 1850.

Washington County, Kentucky. Tax Records: 1829 - 1835.

II. SECONDARY SOURCES

Articles

"History of the Dr. Charles Minor Taylor Memorial," *The
    Junior League of Little Rock, Inc., Area V.,
    Yearbook 1974 - 1975.*

"Philip Trapnall, M.D." Armstrong and Co., *Biographical Encyclopaedia
    of Kentucky, Vol. I.* Cincinnati: n.p., 1878.

Robinson, John V. "Little Rock's Quapaw Quater," *Profile.* Fall, 1968.
    Little Rock, Arkansas.

Ross, Margaret Smith. "Daniel Ringo - Pulaski County Pioneer,'" *Pulaski
    County Historical Review,* September, 1954.

----------. "Sanford C. Faulkner," *The Arkansas Historical Quarterly,*
    14, No. 4. (Winter, 1955).

----------. "Trapnall Hall," *Pulaski County Historical
    Review, December, 1955.*

Stiles, Wilson. "Kentucky Architect First to Design Arkansas
    Building," *The Quapaw Quarter Chronicle.* April, 1978.

Books

Biographical and Historical Memoirs of Central Arkansas.
    Chicago: Goodspeed Publishing Company, 1889.

Cantrell, Ellen H. *Annals of Christ Church Parish from A.D. 1839
    to A.D. 1899.* Little Rock: Arkansas Democrat Co., 1900.

Cocke, Virginia Webb. *Cockes and Cousins, Vol. II: Descendants
    of Thomas Cocke c. 1639 - 1697. Ann Arbor, Michigan:
    Edwards Brothers, Inc., 1974.*

Collins, Richard H. *History of Kentucky from 1543 to January 1, 1874.*
    Louisville, Kentucky: privately printed, 1877.

Daviess, Maria T. *History of Mercer and Boyle Counties, Vol., I.*
    Harrodsburg Kentucky: The Harrodsburg Herald, 1924; reprint 1962.

Hallum, John. *Biographical and Pictorial History of Arkansas, Vol. I.*
    Albany: Weed, Parsons and Company, 1887.

Hempstead, Fay. *Reminiscences of Christ Church: An Addres Delivered
    by Mr. Fay Hempstead, July 20, 1924.*

Herndon, Dallas T. *Highlights of Arkansas History.* n.p.: n.p., 1922.

Johnson, Boyd W. *The Arkansas Frontier.* n.p.: n.p., 1957.

McDonald, Margaret Simms. *White Already to Harvest: TheEpiscopal Church in Arkansas, 1838 - 1971.* Sewanee, Tennessee: University Press, 1975.

Morison, Samuel Eliot. *The Oxford History of the American People.* New York: Oxford University Press, 1965.

Pope, Judge William F. *Early Days in Arkansas.* Little Rock: Frederick W. Allsopp, 1895.

Richards, Ira Don. *Story of a Rivertown: Little Rock in the Nineteenth Century.* Privately printed, 1969.

Shinn, Josiah H. *Pioneers and Makers of Arkansas.* Little Rock, 1908; reprint Baltimore: Genealogical and Historical Publishing Co., 1967.

Webster, Thomas. *An Encyclopaedia of Domestic Economy: Comprising Such Subjects as are more immediately connected with housekeeping: as, The Construction of Domestic Edifices, with the Modes of Warming, Ventilating and Lighting them; A Description of the Various Articles of Furniture: A General Account of the Animal and Vegetable Substances used as food, and the Methods of Preserving and Preparing them by Cooking: Making Bread: Materials employed in Dress and the Toilet: Business of the Laundry: Description of the Various Wheel-Carriages: Preservation of Health; Domestic Medicines, &c., &c.* New York: Harper and Brothers, 1845.

Interviews

Ault, Charles C. Telephone interview. 26 June 1980.

Baltz, Mathias. Telephone interview. 26 June 1980.

Cazort, Allan. Telephone interview. 26 June 1980.

Easley, Edgar J. Telephone interview. 26 June 1980.

King, The Reverend Chester W., Vicar St. Philip's Eposcopal Church, Harrodsburg, Kentucky. Personal interview. 9 August 1979.

Moss, Roger. Personal interview with Barbara Brigance. 17 November 1979.

Robinson, John V. Personal interview. 28 January 1980.

Ross, Margaret Smith. Personal interview. 23 June 1980.

Riley, Warren S. Telephone interview. 26 June 1980.

Smith, Mrs. George Rose (Peg). Personal interview. 2 January 1980.

Stiles, Wilson. Personal interview. 19 April 1980.

Thompson, Francis. Telephone interview. 16 July 1979.

Throgmorton, Howard. Telephone interview. 16 July 1980.

Van Aradsell, Mrs. C. B. Telephone interview. 10 August 1979.

Wirthlin, Mrs. Milton. Telephone interview. 26 June 1980.

Unpublished Works

Austin, Brian (Trapnell Family Historian). Collected Papers.
    Staffordshire, England. manuscript.

Means, Allan O. "F. W. Trapnall, A Historical Monograph," Little
    Rock University. 1 May 1964. typescript.

Street, Mrs. Garland W. "Chicot County Historical Sketch."' Place File,
    Arkansas History Commission, Little Rock, Arkansas. typescript.

Truemper, John J. Jr. "Diary Notes on Trapnall Hall." 6 May 1963 - 10
    September 1963. typescript.

Letters

Austin, Brian (Trapnell Family Historian). Letter to author.
    13 August 1979.

George, Jack. Letter to author. 11 July 1980.

Millard, Roy. Letter to author. 10 July 1980.

Pamphlets

History of St. Philip's Episcopal Church, Short and Chiles
    Streets, Harrodsburg, Kentucky. Privately printed, n.d.

III. MISCELLANEOUS

Abstract of title to Trapnall Place, Beach Abstract and Guaranty
    Company, Little Rock, Arkansas.

Historic Preservation Program. National Register of Historic Places
    Nomination Form, Curran Hall. Prepared by
    Mike Shinn, 9 September 1975.

_____. National Register of Historic Places Nomination Form,
    Trapnall Hall. Prepared by John V. Robinson, 20 October 1972.

Tombstone Inscriptions, Mount Holly Cemetery, Little Rock, Arkansas.